GET YARD SMART

GET YARD SMART

Series Editor
Barbara Loos Chintz

Series Art Director
Barbara Rietschel

Produced by Storey Communications, Inc.,
Pownal, Vermont for Reader's Digest Association, Inc.

Managing Editor
Catherine Gee Graney

Design/Production Editor
Leslie Noyes

Project Manager
Andrea E. Reynolds

Horticultural Editors
Charles W.G. Smith
Elizabeth P. Stell

Editors
Nancy Ondra
Robert Pini

Consultant
Sal Rausa of American Landscapes

Writers
Ronald F. Kujawski
Rosemary McCreary
Laura Tringali
Sara Jane von Trapp

Copyeditor
Gina Grant

Photo Manager
Laurie Geannelis

Picture Research
Mary T. Brott
Laurie Figary
Constance L. King
Amy Richards

Cover Illustration
John Hovell

Cataloging in Publication Data has been applied for from the Library of Congress.

The credits and acknowledgments that appear on pages 168 are hereby made a part of this copyright page.

GET YARD SMART

READER'S DIGEST SMART SERIES™

THE EASY QUICK-START GUIDE TO THE WORKINGS OF YOUR PROPERTY

The Reader's Digest Association, Inc., Pleasantville, New York•Montreal

INTRODUCTION

SMART GUIDE

Smart Guide: At-a-glance directions on placement and planting; with tools and plant parts labeled.

CHECKLIST

Checklist: Steps for easy plant care.

SHORTCUTS

Shortcuts: Ways to save time and/or money.

TROUBLE

Trouble: Tips on common problems and their solutions.

Tackling the yard can be just as stressful, time-consuming, and expensive as working on the house. That's where GET YARD SMART comes in—it takes the mystery and misery out of landscaping and maintaining a yard. This is good news because a well-landscaped yard will improve the value of your home by 20 percent! So before you buy, before you plant, before you do a thing, get the inside track on how your yard works—and what to do when some part of it doesn't. Use the very smart graphic tools shown here to see at a glance just what you need to know.

PLANT SMART

PLANT	HEIGHT	ZONE
Boxwood	15'–20'	
Daylily	1½'–6'	
Pachysandra	8"–12"	
Sugar maple	60'–75'	
Wisteria	to 30'	

Plant Smart: Lets you know where favorite plants will grow best and how tall they'll get.

GARDEN RESOURCES

Aquapore Moisture Systems, Inc. 800-635-8379

Gardener's Supply Company 800-955-3370

Park Seed Company 800-845-3369

Plow & Hearth . . .800-627-1712

Smith & Hawkin 800-776-5558

Spring Hill Nurseries 800-582-8527

Stokes Seeds, Inc. . .716-695-6980

W. Atlee Burpee Co. 800-333-5808

White . . . . Flower Farm 800-503-9624

Resources: Phone numbers of key nurseries, mail order houses, and garden specialty companies.

Feel free to contact us with your thoughts and comments at our Web site:
www.readersdigest.com

TABLE OF CONTENTS

LANDSCAPE DESIGN . . . . 7 to 23
   Make the front, side and backyard work for you.
   Plus info. on driveways, paths. Bonus: The do's
   and don'ts of hiring landscape professionals.

CLIMATE/SUN/SOIL . . . . 25 to 39
   Finally, the basics defined and de-mystified,
   from climate zones to soil, slope, drainage,
   and pesticides.

LAWNS . . . . 41 to 55
   Whether new or existing, get the inside track
   on how to seed, water, mow, and maintain the lawn.

GROUND COVERS . . . . 57 to 65
   Use these little plants to solve your yard
   problems: from steep slopes to shady spots.

TREES . . . . 67 to 79
   Choose from evergreen, shade, flowering, and
   fruit trees and learn how to plant and maintain them.

HEDGES . . . . 81 to 91
   Nature's own idea of fencing can be yours.
   Learn about privacy, boundary, and hostile hedges.

FLOWERING SHRUBS . . . . 93 to 105
   Jazz up your house with these pretty
   decorative shrubs: hydrangeas, azaleas, viburnums,
   shrub roses, and more.

EASY FLOWERS . . . . .107 to 123
   Start out with annuals, graduate to bulbs,
   and when you're ready, try your hand at
   perennials. A smart way to beautify your yard.

SPECIALTY GARDENS . . . . .125 to 139
   Terrific accents for almost any yard. Try a
   water garden, a rock garden, or a container
   garden.

PATIOS/DECKS/POOLS . . . . .141 to 161
   All the toys of the yard explained, from pools
   and patios to decks and kids' play areas.

INDEXES & PHOTO CREDITS . . . . .162 to 168

LANDSCAPE DESIGN

Chances are either you're starting from scratch (a newly built house with no plantings whatsoever) or you want to improve on what you've got (get rid of overgrown plants or maybe replace a walkway). Dreaming up your ideal yard can be fun. Here are some basic pointers to help turn your dreams into reality.

SMART GUIDE...8/9

PLANNING AND DESIGN 10/11

FRONT YARD 12/13

SIDE YARD 14/15

BACKYARD 16/17

WALKWAYS 18/19

DRIVEWAYS...20/21

LANDSCAPE PROFESSIONALS 22/23

LANDSCAPE DESIGN

To get smart about landscape design, use this easy number guide to identify and name parts of a landscape blueprint. More detailed explanations follow in this chapter.

SITE INVENTORY

1 . . . HOUSE (in bold)

2 . . . GARAGE (in bold)

3 . . . DRIVEWAY

4 . . . SEPTIC TANK

5 . . . LEACH FIELD

6 . . . SWING SET

7 . . . EASEMENTS (for electric and water)

8 . . . PROPERTY LINES

9 . . . WATER LINE

10 . . . ELECTRIC SERVICE

MASTER PLAN

11 . . . TOPOGRAPHY LINES (each line indicates 2 feet more of slope)

12 . . . STARTING POINT FOR SETTING SLOPE

13 . . . EXISTING LAWN

14 . . . EXISTING TREES (unlabeled)

15 . . . NEW FRONT WALKWAY

16 . . . NEW BACK DECK

17 . . . NEW TERRACE/PATIO

18 . . . NEW TREES (labeled)

19 . . . NEW FOUNDATION PLANTS (labeled)

20 . . . NEW SHRUBS (labeled)

LEGEND

21 . . . COMPASS

22 . . . ARCHITECT'S GENERAL CONSTRUCTION NOTES

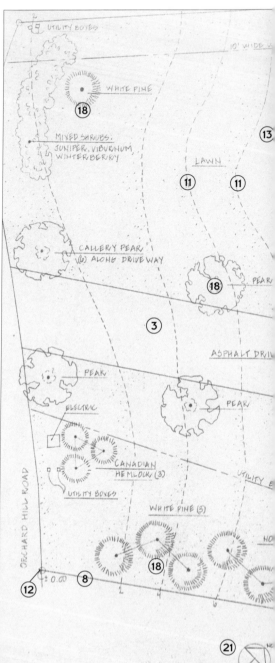

CREATING A LANDSCAPE MASTER PLAN

A master plan is a blueprint of how new plants and hardscapes (walkways, patios, etc.) will look with what you've got now. To create one, hire a landscape architect or designer to draw one for you. Most charge a flat fee, some work by the hour. Among other other things, the master plan will include a list of all new plants (with both Latin and common names). This list will be the basis of the bid from the landscape contractor. Depending on the extent of the work, the length of the planting season, and your budget, landscape architects and designers may deal with only one area of the yard a season. In this case, each new phase will probably require a more specific "detail" drawing, usually for an additional fee.

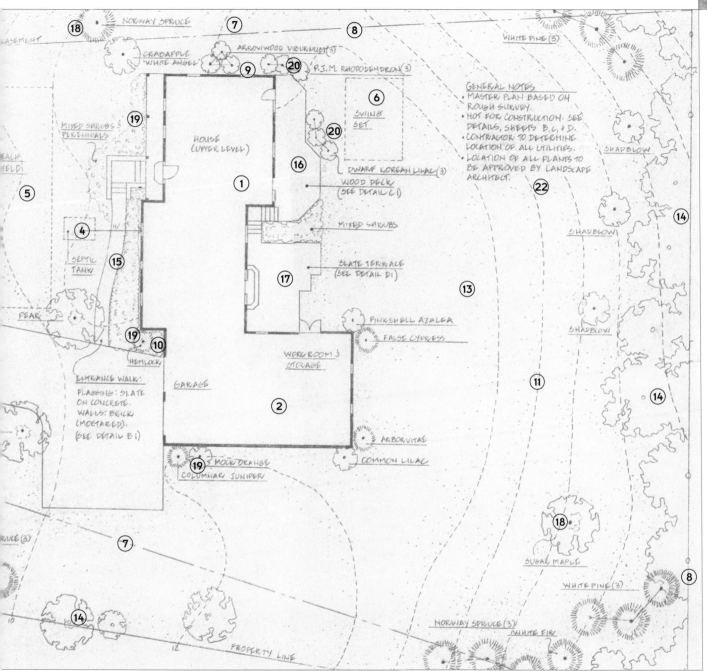

NORWAY SPRUCE

18 7 8

BASEMENT

WHITE PINE (3)

CRABAPPLE
'WHITE ANGEL'

ARROWWOOD VIBURNUM (3)

9 20 P.J.M. RHODODENDRON (3)

6
SWING
SET

19 SHADBLOW

MIXED SHRUBS
PERENNIALS

HOUSE
(UPPER LEVEL)

20

BEACH
FIELD

16

DWARF KOREAN LILAC (3)

1 WOOD DECK
(SEE DETAIL C)

5

14

4

MIXED SHRUBS

SHADBLOW

SEPTIC
TANK

15 SLATE TERRACE
(SEE DETAIL D)

22

17

13

PEAR

SHADBLOW

PINKSHELL AZALEA

FALSE CYPRESS

19 10
HEMLOCK

11

ENTRANCE WALK:

FLAGGING: SLATE
ON CONCRETE.
WALLS: BRICK
(MORTARED).
(SEE DETAIL B)

GARAGE

WORK ROOM &
STORAGE

2

ARBORVITAE

14

COMMON LILAC

19 MOCK ORANGE
COLUMNAR JUNIPER

SPRUCE (3)

7

18

SUGAR MAPLE

14

WHITE PINE (3)

8

NORWAY SPRUCE (3)
WHITE FIR

PROPERTY LINE

PLANNING AND DESIGN

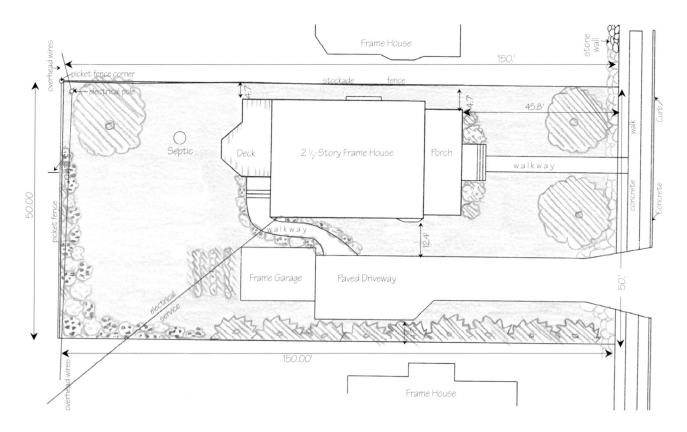

Make copies of your home survey and draw your ideas on them. The survey will give you the dimensions of your property and the location of immovable items, such as the electrical line or the septic tank.

You don't have to tackle your whole property at once. Do what the landscape professionals do and divide it into three basic elements: front yard, side yard, and backyard. The front yard is considered a public space to welcome visitors; the side yard is usually a utility area for toolsheds, trash cans, and so on; while the backyard is for private family fun—cookouts, games, hot tubs, lounging. Use walkways to tie these spaces together.

If you are clueless about what you want in your front, back-, or side yard,

take a walk in your neighborhood and note what you find appealing. First, do you like formal- or informal-looking yards? Formal yards are symmetrical, with plants forming right angles, and hedges neatly clipped. Informal yards are more casual, with curved flower beds, winding walkways, and trees set at oblique angles.

Now go back home and look at the shape and the style of your house. Geometric and formal houses (Georgian and Colonial) do well with the straight lines of formal designs. Informal, asymmetrical houses (some moderns and ranches) beg for a more informal landscape, with curving paths and lush, free-form plantings. Note: Formal gardens require more maintenance (weeding and trimming) than informal gardens do.

Next, think about existing features you'd like to change, or additions you have always wanted. Need to enlarge the driveway? Want to put in a flower bed? How about cutting down on yard maintenance and replacing the lawn with a ground cover?

Keep in mind that the changes you want to make will need to fit the existing conditions of your yard. That means understanding how your local climate, soil, and amount of light affect your yard. (See the next chapter, "Climate/Sun/Soil," for information.)

For a fast, informed design solution, hire a landscape designer or architect (see page 22). You will still have to figure out what you want, but it's helpful to have an expert's input from the get-go. Note: You can complete your new design in stages, over a period of time. Just bear in mind how long you plan to own your home. Plants you put in now should provide enjoyment and reach maturity before you want to sell.

CHECKLIST

LANDSCAPE PLANNING

✔ Before you start dreaming, know where your power lines, water lines, septic tank, and phone and cable lines are located.

✔ Involve your whole family in the design process—especially when creating your wish list. Don't forget to include the kids.

✔ Look at existing patterns of foot and vehicle traffic in your yard, and plan new paths and driveways accordingly. It's easier to change the landscape than to change people's walking and driving habits.

✔ Look out your windows to see how the landscape will look from inside. Measure from the ground to each windowsill so that you know how tall plants can grow before blocking the view.

✔ Take photos of your existing plants at each season so that you'll know how your existing plants will fit into your new plans.

✔ If you're not sure which colors you want, start with green foliage and a single color for flowers and shrubs.

✔ To spread expenses out, create a three-, five-, or seven-year plan for implementing your new landscape; make adjustments as ideas change.

When landscaping near your house, try to camouflage the straight lines of the house with the rounded, softer shapes of plants. Here, a tree softens the roof line, and a mixture of shrubs and perennials modifies the gutter and foundation lines.

FRONT YARD

Soften the edges of a walkway with a border of flowers; here, the main walkway features 1) yellow melampodium. 2) White geraniums line the walkway at right, by side door.

Your front yard is the public face of your home, so make it welcoming. How? For starters, be sure the entrance is clearly marked with 1) easy-to-read address numbers and 2) safe and accessible walkways and steps to the front door. Note: The front walkway should be wide enough for two people to walk side by side—at least 4' wide. The wider the front steps, the more gracious and inviting the effect.

When it comes to landscaping, the goal is to harmonize plants with your house. One easy way to do this is with foundation plants. These, typically low evergreen shrubs, are planted around the perimeter of the house. They get their name because they hide the foundation (the masonry wall that you see on some houses that ranges from 1' to 6' up from the ground). Nowadays, foundation plants may extend beyond the line along the house foundation to tie the lawn and the house together.

Some foundation-plant pointers: 1) Avoid plants that will grow too tall and block windows; 2) because of their high visibility, go for plants that look good most of the year—try evergreen shrubs (see pages 98–101), ornamental grasses (see page 64), or perennial flowers (see page 118); 3) keep 1' of space between the house and the plants to keep your house free of bugs and moisture.

PLANNING SMART

✔Look at your yard from across the street or from the road to check the perspective. What do arriving visitors see? What stands out?

✔Know where power, water, and sewer lines are located.

✔Plan the main walkway to the house to widen where it meets the driveway and the front stoop; this will make it more inviting.

✔Install the hardscape (that's the walkway and the steps, in the landscape business) before adding any plants to your front yard. You could damage the plantings during construction if you don't.

✔Homes with just a few inches of exposed foundation may not need anything to hide it; low-growing ground covers add welcoming color and accent the house with little or no work at all.

✔To keep pruning to a minimum, plant dwarf trees (see page 76) as foundation plantings.

✔Break up a large front lawn with a specimen plant (these stand alone), such as a particularly beautiful shrub, a single tree, or a clump of ornamental grass (see page 64).

TROUBLE

• More than 6' of exposed foundation? Create a raised planter in front by building a low retaining wall of stone, wood, or concrete. Fill with topsoil and plant it with plants that will cascade over the edge.

• Steep slope? Build two or more low walls with railroad ties or stones to create level areas. Fill these terraces with plants.

• Two front doors? Target the primary entrance by making its path and steps wider. Minimize the family entryway by constructing a narrower walkway or by planting shrubs or trees to block it from view.

Plant large trees at least 30' from the house to prevent roots from encroaching and limbs from falling on the house when trees reach maturity.

SIDE YARD

A gate or an arbor (see page 148) between the side yard and the back-yard will separate the two areas and allow you to create two different types of gardens.

The lowly side yard usually receives the least respect. It's usually either a way to get from the front yard to the back or a place to stash the trash cans, woodpile, and clothesline. You can rescue your side yard from its mundane functional duties and turn it into something that's both useful and appealing.

Start by determining your utility needs. A small shed is handy for storing garden tools and freeing up garage space. With a little paint and trim, a tool-shed (see page 158) can serve as a garden feature as well as a storage spot.

Need space to store firewood or compost bins? Put them behind the shed or install a small fence to keep them out of sight. Use the posts of clotheslines as supports for climbing vines.

After the practical issues are settled, it's time to have fun. If your side yard is like many and gets only limited sun, choose shade-loving plants. In long, narrow yards, put large plants in the center and small plants at either end. Narrow spaces look wider when you add curved paths or winding flower beds.

A little-used side yard is a great place to create a vegetable or herb garden, provided it gets six hours of full sun a day. A few rows of 1) cucumbers, 2) Swiss chard, 3) tomatoes, and 4) squash are easy to care for and delicious to eat. 5) Marigolds help keep pests away from the vegetables while adding bright color.

With special pruning and tying, this pear tree will spread its branches horizontally against the fence. This technique of espalier (ask about it at your local nursery) allows you to grow a fruit tree in a narrow side yard.

SHORTCUTS

• Plan pathways through the side yard for easy access to compost bins, trash cans, and other frequently visited spots. Make paths flat and easy to walk on. Stepping-stones are nice.

• Piles of firewood can become homes to pests like mice, termites, or carpenter ants. Store firewood at least 2' from the sides of the house.

• Construct sheds and other storage containers (see page 158) with materials similar to your house siding to give the area a unified look. Or paint them dark green to help them blend into surrounding shrubby areas.

• Side yards are excellent spots for specialty gardens, such as container gardens (see page 134) and kitchen gardens (see page 136).

BIRD GARDENS

Turn an ungainly side yard into a bird-watcher's paradise by installing a bird feeder, birdhouse, and birdbath. In larger gardens, add a mixture of shrubs and trees. Try small deciduous trees, such as serviceberry, dogwood (see page 74), crab apple, and mountain ash, and evergreens like weeping hemlock, and blue and dwarf Alberta spruce (see page 72). Mix with such fruit-producing shrubs as viburnum (see page 100), cotoneaster, winged euonymus, winterberry, and juniper. These will provide food, shelter, and nesting space to entice winged creatures.

A bluebird house will help attract these colorful songbirds.

BACKYARD

Large trees can provide shade, screening, and privacy in a yard. Fences, flower beds, and features like the gazebo, center, can create interesting focal points.

The backyard is your outdoor living room. Depending on your interests, it may have a patio, playground, flower beds, barbecue, or picnic area—maybe even a swimming pool. Whew! How to make it all fit?

One easy design trick is to divide the backyard into specialty areas. How much you entertain will help determine the size of your deck; how often and what type of games you play will tell you how much lawn you need. Don't forget to anticipate future needs—what serves as a children's play area now can be replaced by gardens, or a pool or lawn, when the kids are older.

In a big yard, you might use fences or hedges to separate the space into various smaller areas for different activities. When space is at a premium, try features that will meet two or more needs. A well-planned deck or patio, for instance, may serve for both entertaining and container gardening (see page 134). A single garden can be designed to hold a mix of flowers, vegetables, and herbs, so you won't need three separate gardens.

Think also about screening the yard with a fence (see page 144) or a hedge (see page 81) for privacy from the neighbors.

Forgo the lawn if space is scarce and slopes make mowing difficult or dangerous. Here, plants that grow well on a hillside form a frame for the brick patio.

SHORTCUTS • Before building anything, whether a toolshed or a deck, contact your local building department or zoning board; you may need a permit.

• Place children's play areas where they can easily be viewed through windows; you can keep an eye on the youngsters from inside. Install temporary fencing around play yards.

• Locate flower beds in those areas of the backyard that immediately catch your eye. If you aren't sure what color flowers to plant, start with white. It's simple and elegant. Use annuals to try out a different second and third color each year. (See page 110.)

• Lawns make backyards look bigger.

TROUBLE • Need to hide electric junction boxes, meters, gas tanks, or other unattractive features? Use plantings that blend in with the surroundings and don't call attention to themselves.

• Tired of soccer balls in your flower beds? A low picket fence around the garden adds interest and keeps the plants in and the stray balls out.

• Backyard on a steep slope? Create terraces for gardens; build a multilevel deck.

• Noisy neighbors? Block out noise with dense privacy hedges (see page 84).

WALKWAYS

Straight paths can seem severe. Soften them with irregularly shaped drifts of flowers. This path features several different types of 1) dianthus, mixed with 2) creeping thyme, and 3) moss phlox, plus a few violas.

Let the design of your house guide the shape of walkways and choice of materials. Paths with straight edges will complement a formal style of architecture. Regularly shaped materials, such as bricks and flagstones, lend themselves to these orderly walkways. Informal designs call for curves and often combine different materials.

High-traffic paths need durable materials: brick, interlocking pavers, or concrete. Exposed aggregate (concrete with pebbles pressed into the surface) offers more style and offers the easy-care quality and solidity of plain concrete. For less traveled tracks, gravel or wood chips create a welcoming path. A series of stepping-stones can turn a worn, muddy trail through the side yard into a pretty path. Shredded bark, pine needles, and even sawdust make natural-looking pathways through and around garden areas. Note: Main walkways need to be 4' to 5' wide to accommodate two people walking side by side. Secondary paths can be narrower; 2' is fine.

Don't forget about plants. Line your walkway with ground-hugging plants to add color and texture to a plain old walkway. Choose from SWEET ALYSSUM (an annual), CREEPING THYME, DALMATIAN BELL-FLOWER, and MOSS PHLOX.

• Use crushed gravel to create a quick, inexpensive path for the side yard and back of the house. To control weeds layer plastic or, better, landscape fabric (available at garden centers) on the path first, then cover with gravel.

• Preformed stepping-stones are great for secondary paths. Note: If placed in lawns, they need lots of edge trimming, so keep them for short paths.

• Match steps' material to the path material so they don't stick out like a sore thumb. If you have wood steps, cover the path leading to them with wood or bark chips.

• To make a more formal path, frame with heavy timbers, railroad ties, brick, or stone, then fill with gravel or wood chips.

• Ramps allow easier access for people who use wheelchairs. Make a ramp with an 8 percent slope (a rise of 8" for every 100" of distance) and add a safe, nonskid surface.

• Tracking path material into the house? Don't use fine, loose material—shredded bark, pine needles, and sawdust—on paths that lead to the back or front door.

• Path edges crumbling? Installing a sturdy metal or plastic edging strip keeps bricks and pavers in place. (The strips are available at most garden centers.) Vinyl or wood strips work well for holding gravel, wood chips, and other loose materials in place.

A gentle curve softens the look of a standard concrete front path. Flower beds close to the house issue an invitation to come and visit.

Colored concrete interlocking pavers give this small side yard walkway a nice texture.

PLANT SMART

PLANT	HEIGHT	ZONE
Creeping thyme	3"–6"	
Dalmatian bellflower	6"	
Moss phlox	4"	
Sweet alyssum	3"–6"	

WALKWAY SOURCES

Backyard Products. 814-455-0074

Halquist Stone Company 414-246-3561

Milestones 425-882-1987

Mister Boardwalk 800-813-4050

Paveloc Industries 800-590-2772

Sierra Jane's Trading Company. 410-740-2984

DRIVEWAYS

This wide asphalt driveway is perked up with colorful plantings of double-flowered annual poppies.

Driveways can actually beckon the visitor, not just serve as a passageway from the road. But to achieve that curbside appeal, good design has to create some soft edges along a very hard place.

Some basic considerations: the width of your driveway will depend on the number and size of the cars in your household. (For each car, you'll need 12' wide x 24' long of driveway.) Circular drives make movement easier but take up more space than straight ones. A turnaround that juts out from the drive takes up less room.

Walkways from the house to the driveway should complement the driveway. Try to use materials that are similar in color or tone (for example, a redbrick walkway with a red gravel driveway; a fieldstone path with an asphalt drive).

It's tempting to plant flowers or shrubs to line a driveway, but this can be a headache to maintain if you have a narrow driveway; and a misjudged turn or an errant snowplow will lay waste to your plantings. Unless you have a wide driveway, leave a strip of grass at least 2' wide on each side, then plant a flower border beyond that. Keep shrubs and trees at least 6' to 8' away from the edges of the driveway. (In cold climates, leave room on either side of the driveway to pile snow so that it doesn't harm shrubs and perennials.)

Brick paving defines an extra parking area but looks like it's part of the walkway.

Stamped concrete edged with flowers.

DRIVEWAY-SURFACE MATERIALS

Here are the pros and cons of the materials commonly used for driveway surfaces:

GRAVEL AND SURE-PACK (a mixture of different sizes of gravel)—Pro: Low cost; aesthetically appealing. Con: Requires fresh gravel every few years; may lose gravel when shoveling snow.

ASPHALT—Pro: Easy to maintain and easy to clear of snow. Con: Can crack; needs to be resealed every three to four years.

CONCRETE—Pro: Very durable. Have it stamped (or cut) for a decorative look. Con: Can develop cracks; should have a masonry sealer applied every year, especially in cold climates. Shows oil stains.

PRECAST CONCRETE PAVERS—Pro: Very durable, and available in many shapes and colors. They withstand at least 2,000 pounds of pressure per square inch, so cars and snowplows will not damage them. Con: Expensive to install.

SHORTCUTS
• To add parking to a straight driveway, widen it. Determine how many cars you need to accommodate and multiply that number by 12' for width. Allow at least 24' in length.

• Create an overflow parking area next to your driveway with turfstones—concrete blocks with pockets for soil and grass. Once they're installed, the grass will hide the concrete framing.

TROUBLE
• Snowplow service wreaking havoc? Mark driveway edges with stakes topped with orange paint reflectors for nighttime visibility. And tell the snowplower where to pile snow to avoid plantings and trees.

• Driveway-edging timbers disheveled? Overlap them in Lincoln Log fashion.

• Puddles forming on your gravel driveway? Watch out for low spots and fill in with extra gravel as soon as they form to avoid rutting and erosion.

DRIVEWAY-SURFACE SOURCES

Gardener Asphalt Corporation. . . . 813-248-2101

Gibson Honans 800-433-7293

Halquist Stone Company. 414-246-3561

Paveloc Industries. 800-590-2772

Rocks, Etc. Inc. 815-836-0086

Uni-Group USA. 800-872-1864

LANDSCAPE PROFESSIONALS

The hardscape elements—a path and a wall, for example—are usually installed first. Plantings like flower beds and shrubs are added around them.

How hard can it be to redo a yard? Depends on what you're doing. Big plans (removing trees and shrubs, putting down a new lawn, planting a hedge) definitely require professional help. Small projects, like planting a flower bed or shrubs, you will probably be able to handle on your own—if you want to. Otherwise, call in the pros.

There are several types of landscaping professionals to choose from. The most highly trained are landscape architects. They can create a design that incorporates all the elements of a yard, from hardscape (decks and patios) to the plantings, to add value to your property. Landscape designers' expertise lies with plants; they may not have as much know-how about the hardscape. Note: For either profession, not all states require licensing.

Landscape contractors (the people who actually do the work) can also be landscape designers. In general, contractors make their profit on the installation end of the job and may be willing to discount the price of a landscape plan in order to get the installation.

To work with a landscape professional, first determine your budget. A landscape architect or designer charges fees either as a percentage of the job or by an hourly rate not to exceed a set limit. If you hire a landscape professional to oversee the implementation of the design, he or she will then bid-out and oversee all phases of the contracting work. Be sure to get the design work finished over the winter for an early-spring start on construction.

HIRING HELP

✔ Ask for referrals. If you see a landscape you like, ask the homeowners who did the design work, how long it has been in place, and what their experience was. Was the contractor reliable and easy to communicate with; did he/she stay within budget? Clean up each day? Have courteous workers?

✔ Get bids from three professionals whose work you've seen either in person or in pictures and whose jobs have been in place for at least three years. Throw out the lowest bid and take a serious look at the differences between the two other proposals.

✔ Work with a contractor who gives you some form of written proposal, plan, or contract, which you both sign.

✔ Ask for proof of insurance before a contractor sets foot on your property.

✔ There should be no surprises. Your contractor or designer should work within a pre-set budget. If you want more than you can afford, ask the contractor or designer to phase the project so that you can complete the work over a few seasons or years.

✔ Ask about guarantees. It's common practice to guarantee new plants for one year.

✔ For tree work, you will need to hire a tree service. They usually have an arborist (tree specialist) on staff who will inspect your trees for damage and come up with a maintenance plan for pruning, fertilizing, and cabling trees.

✔ Basic lawn care is also available for hire. Local firms offer weekly to monthly maintenance plans—everything from fertilizing in the spring and cutting the lawn all summer to raking leaves in the fall (see page 53).

FENG SHUI

For landscape design with a sense of harmony, contact a Feng Shui consultant, who will assess the flow of energy on your property. He or she will evaluate if the plants, light, water, wind, and sound in your yard are creating positive or negative energy. Negative energy usually flows in straight lines, so Feng Shui solutions will emphasize curved forms—for example, winding pathways, water gardens, and plantings that create interesting sight lines. Whatever the spiritual benefits of a Feng Shui design, you'll be sure to have a pleasing landscape.

Water features are often used to create positive energy flow.

Major landscape work calls for heavy equipment. Your landscape professional should be able to coordinate all phases of the work.

PROFESSIONAL RESOURCES

American Feng
Shui Institute. 626-571-2757

Associated Landscape
Contractors of
America 703-736-9666

Association of
Professional Landscape
Designers 312-201-0101

Feng Shui
Warehouse. 800-399-1599

Landscape Architect
Foundation. 202-898-2444

National Arborist
Association Inc. . . . 800-733-2622

Professional Lawncare
Association of
America 770-977-5222

CLIMATE/SUN/ SOIL

Having a green thumb in the garden—instead of being all thumbs—starts with learning what you've got to work with. That means knowing about the climate you live in, the amount of light your yard gets, and the type of soil you've got. Read on and find out how a little technical expertise can go a long way.

SMART GUIDE.....................................26/27

CLIMATE ZONES...............................28/29

THE ELEMENTS.................................30/31

SOIL 32/33

SOIL pH/FERTILIZER..........................34/35

DRAINAGE 36/37

WEED/PEST CONTROL......................38/39

CLIMATE/SUN/SOIL

To get smart about climate, sun, and soil, use this easy number guide to identify how these factors affect conditions in your yard. Detailed explanations follow in this chapter.

CLIMATE/ELEMENTS/SOIL

1 . . . FIND OUT YOUR CLIMATE ZONE

2 . . . NOTE PATTERNS OF SUN AND SHADE

3 . . . FIGURE OUT WIND DIRECTION

4 . . . TEST SOIL TYPE

5 . . . TEST SOIL pH (from various parts of yard)

6 . . . IMPROVE SOIL IF NECESSARY (not shown)

7 . . . FERTILIZE TREES AND OTHER PLANTINGS

8 . . . PLANT TREES OR HEDGE (for windbreak)

9 . . . LOW AREAS CREATE COLD SPOTS (plant hardy plants here)

10 . . . SHELTERED AREAS CREATE WARM SPOTS (use less hardy plants here)

DRAINAGE

11 . . . CHECK GRADE AROUND HOUSE FOR PROPER DRAINAGE

12 . . . IMPROVE GRADE IF NECESSARY

13 . . . CHECK FOR WET AREAS (at low points and bases of slopes)

14 . . . INSTALL DRAINAGE PIPE IN WET AREAS, OR PLANT WATER GARDEN

WEED/PEST CONTROL

15 . . . COVER FLOWER BEDS WITH MULCH (to prevent weeds)

16 . . . SPACE PLANTS (to allow good air circulation)

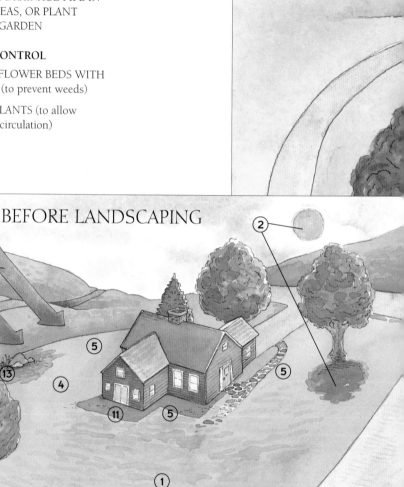

BEFORE LANDSCAPING

AFTER LANDSCAPING

CLIMATE ZONES

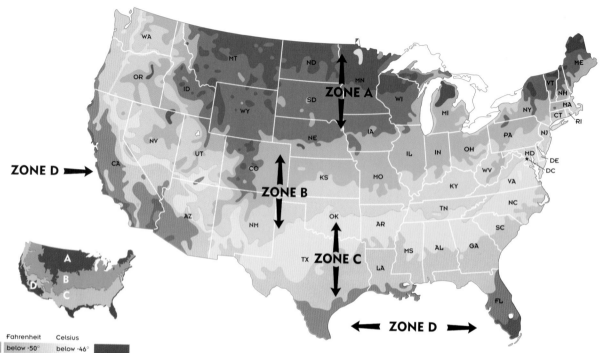

	Fahrenheit	Celsius	
Zone 1	below -50°	below -46°	
Zone 2	-50° to -40°	-46° to -40°	ZONE A
Zone 3	-40° to -30°	-40° to -34°	
Zone 4	-30° to -20°	-34° to -29°	
Zone 5	-20° to -10°	-29° to -23°	ZONE B
Zone 6	-10° to 0°	-23° to -18°	
Zone 7	0° to 10°	-18° to -12°	ZONE C
Zone 8	10° to 20°	-12° to -7°	
Zone 9	20° to 30°	-7° to -1°	
Zone 10	30° to 40°	-1° to 4°	ZONE D
Zone 11	above 40°	above 4°	

This color key shows the average minimum winter temperature for each of the USDA climate zones. In Get Yard Smart, we have made this information easier to use by condensing the 11 zones into 4. Plant Smart boxes in this book use blue to represent USDA Zones 1–4, green for Zones 5–6, gold for Zones 7–8, and red for Zones 9–11.

Like hardy people, hardy plants can weather tough climates. In plant-land, hardiness means how much cold a plant can survive.

To help you pick plants that will survive in your local climate, the U.S. Department of Agriculture has divided the United States and Canada into 11 different climate zones, each with its own average minimum and maximum temperature. Zone 1 in upper Canada is the coldest; zone 11 in southern Florida and California is the warmest. Most plants you buy will come with a tag noting either one zone, say 3, or a range of zones, say 3 to 8, which means the plant can sur-

vive the cold temperatures of zone 3 and hot temperatures up through zone 8. Knowing your local zone will ensure that the plants you buy will survive.

Don't be surprised if areas in your yard are slightly warmer or colder. Temperatures can vary depending on the amount of wind and sun your yard gets. Windy, open spots will be colder than a sunny corner—for example, where the house meets a stone wall. These little "microclimates" allow you to try plants from one zone higher or lower.

 WINTERIZING
YOUR PLANTS

✔ Before the first freeze, give all your plants a good soaking so that during a winter thaw, they will find melted water.

✔ After the first killing frost, put an extra layer of mulch around the bases of shrubs and perennial flowers to insulate the roots, hold in moisture, regulate temperature, and prevent temperature extremes. Remove the extra mulch in spring so that the roots don't suffocate during the growing season.

✔ When the temperature starts to plunge below freezing, wrap broad-leaved evergreens, such as boxwood (see page 84), with burlap. Remove the covering in spring as soon as the temperatures are reliably above freezing, so the plants don't "cook" under the wrap.

✔ Encircle needle-leaved evergreens with rope to keep their limbs from breaking under heavy snow. Start at the bottom and circle six or seven times until you reach the top.

Burlap is used to protect shrubs from winter sun and wind. Protect plants on southern exposures with wind screens made of burlap tacked to wooden stakes and those on eastern, western, and northern exposures with burlap wraps, as shown above.

 • The higher up you live in the hills or mountains, the colder the climate. You lose a full hardiness zone to the north for every 3,300' of added elevation.

• Low areas in a yard tend to collect cold air and are apt to be "frost pockets," areas that freeze before the rest of your yard does. Grow only extrahardy plants in low spots.

• Snow is an excellent insulator. If your garden is covered with snow for most of the winter, your plants will have an easier time surviving. An extra layer of mulch is a good substitute if snow doesn't cover your yard for most of the winter.

A stone wall near a building can create a sheltered microclimate. If the space faces south, it's a perfect place to plant marginally hardy plants. If it faces north, it will be even colder than the rest of the yard.

THE ELEMENTS

Late-day light angles across a lawn but does not reach the flower bed in front. Plant carefully to match plants' light needs with the amount of sunlight they will get.

You can't change the amount of light and wind your yard gets, so you might as well work with what you've got. Start by watching the sun patterns in your yard to see how much exposure plants will receive. *Full sun* means at least six hours of direct sunlight, usually between the hours of 9 A.M. and 5 P.M. *Partial sun* (also known as partial shade) means four hours of direct sunlight. (Note: Yards with lots of tree branches will get filtered or dappled light, which is considered partial sun.) Finally, *shade* means less than four hours of direct sunlight a day.

Whether a plant needs full sun, partial sun, or shade is stated on most plant identification tags. Plants that prefer sun will reach for light and become "leggy" (long and spindly) if they don't get enough. Alternatively, shade lovers don't have inherent protection from the strong rays of the sun; if exposed, their leaves will burn or discolor.

Few plants like the wind. It is drying, and windchill can be murderous on half-hardy and tender plants (see page 110). The top of a hill can be especially windy. To diminish excessive wind put up a fence as a windbreak. The fence can be an evergreen hedge (see page 81) or a stockade-type wooden fence (see page 144.) The effect is the same—they slow down wind speed.

The tall, closely spaced slats of this stockade fence (above left) make it sturdy enough to act as a windbreak. Snapdragons thrive in bright, sunny places, as shown below, but become weak and spindly (above right) when grown in places that receive only an hour or two of light.

SHORTCUTS • Grass does not like shade. A surefire sign of too much shade for a lawn is a healthy stand of moss. Grow ground covers (see page 57) in those areas and stop fighting Mother Nature.

• If lots of trees create too much shade in your yard, let in more light by removing lower tree branches.

• Mildew and other fungi enjoy the shade and moisture of northern exposures. To discourage their growth, provide good air circulation by pruning shrubs and trees (see pages 68 and 94) and planting away from the walls of buildings.

• Winter winds can dry out evergreen shrubs and trees. Consider spraying them with a protective "antidesiccant" spray, available at most nurseries.

• Avoid planting in areas where wind is tunneled between buildings. The increased speed and intensity of the wind is hard on plants.

• Near the ocean, winds can be especially drying because they carry salt spray. If you want to plant a living windbreak, ask your nursery to recommend salt-tolerant shrubs.

These healthy snapdragons were planted in the right light.

CLIMATE/SUN/SOIL   31

SOIL

Sandy soil 1) is usually light in color and does not clump. Good loamy soil 2) looks dark, rich, and crumbly. Clay soil 3) is clumpy, heavy, and, when dry, can be as hard as cement.

Sand, clay, or silt? Why bother finding out? Because knowing your soil's texture will tell you how well your soil holds on to water and nutrients. *Sandy soil* is very loose, so water (and therefore nutrients) drains through very easily, making the soil not very fertile. *Clay soil* holds so much water there is little room for air. That means poor drainage, but the soil is rich in nutrients. *Silt soil* is in between sandy and clay. *Loamy soil* is a blend of the three.

What do you do if the texture of your soil is too coarse or fine? You fix it by adding organic matter—mix in lots of compost (rotted vegetable matter) or well-rotted cow manure—available at garden centers. These "soil conditioners" will help sandy soil hold on to nutrients and water. Not up for using compost or manure? You can use peat moss, but it makes soil more acidic (see page 34).

For a slower but easier solution, use mulch. Hard mulches, such as bark nuggets or wood chips (available at garden centers), take longer to break down than soft mulches (lawn clippings, chopped leaves), so you won't have to replenish them as often. Spread 2" to 3" of hard mulch around shrubs and trees. Scatter 2" to 3" of soft mulch around annuals (see page 110) and vegetables.

Earthworms are your sign of soil success. By burrowing around, these little guys improve your soil's drainage and aeration. Organic matter supplies earthworms with food, so add lots to entice them to stick around.

SOIL MAKEOVER
✔ You can improve your soil at any time of year as long as it isn't soggy or bone dry. Just spread 3" of organic matter over the soil and mix into the top 6" of soil. Use a garden fork (like a pitchfork) to mix it in.

✔ Don't dig your soil when it squishes underfoot or if you squeeze a handful and it forms a muddy ball—you could damage your soil by creating permanent hard clods. Let the soil dry out until just moist.

✔ If you're improving a large area, rent a rotary tiller, or rototiller (a machine that turns soil), or hire a landscape contractor to do the job (see page 22).

✔ If you're making a new garden, first remove sod (grass with roots and soil) with a spade. This will keep grass from resprouting in your garden.

✔ Create your own compost by saving such throwaways as vegetable scraps, coffee grounds, tea bags, grass clippings, and leaves. Once a week pour in a little water or leftover coffee or tea. Note: Don't put in any animal products (including dairy) or weeds. Don't feel like making your own? Buy compost in bags at your local garden center.

TROUBLE • Using your backyard as a temporary driveway? Don't. Driving a car or other heavy machinery on soil, especially wet soil, will ruin the texture and make it nearly impossible for anything to penetrate it, including plant roots.

• Soil really rocky or soggy? Fixing it will be very expensive. Instead, plant what will accept your conditions. Rock gardens (see page 130) and container gardens (see page 134) convert difficult yards into splendors.

Buy a simple compost bin. Every 10 lb. of kitchen and yard scraps turns into 1 lb. of compost.

COMPOST-BIN SOURCES

Gardeners Eden 800-822-1214

Gardener's Supply Company 800-876-5520

Gurney's Seed & Nursery Co. 605-665-1671

Lee Valley Tools Ltd. 800-871-8158

MULCH SOURCES

Far West Forests 800-334-1930

Lester's Material Service Inc. 847-223-7000

Vermont Maple Mulch 888-50-MULCH

SOIL-CONDITIONER SOURCES

Aimcor Consumer Products LLC . . . 800-207-6457

Earthgro 800-736-7645

Gardeners Supply Company 800-876-5520

Lester's Material Service Inc. 847-223-7000

TWO EASY SOIL TESTS

Test the texture of your soil: grab a handful of moist soil and squeeze. If it crumbles, it's sandy; if it's clumpy and sticky, it's clay; and if it forms a spongy ball that breaks apart easily, it's loamy or silty.

To test how well your soil drains, dig a hole 1' wide by 1' deep in your garden. Fill the hole with water. It should drain in an hour or two. If it drains faster than that, your soil is too sandy. If it takes longer to drain, say up to 24 hours, then your soil is too heavy (has too much clay or is too packed down). The cure is the same for both: lots of organic matter.

SOIL pH/FERTILIZER

Why test the pH of your soil? Because if the pH (level of acidity or alkalinity) is too high or too low, your plants will not be able to absorb nutrients from the soil—no matter how much fertilizer you pour on.

A brief chemistry refresher: the level of acidity or alkalinity is measured on a scale of 1 to 14, with 7 being neutral. A pH below 7 means the soil is acidic, a pH above 7 means the soil is alkaline. In general, a slightly acid pH of between 6 and 7 is best for most plants. Test your soil using either a soil kit or calling your local Cooperative Extension Service, which will do a more accurate test for you.

If your soil's pH is out of whack, you will need to "amend," or alter, your soil. How? By mixing in chemicals, so-called soil amendments. For instance, to lower the pH of a highly alkaline soil, add powdered sulfur or aluminum sulfate. To amend a highly acid soil, add limestone or lots of wood ashes. Your soil test will tell you how much you need, or you can hire a landscape contractor (see page 22) to handle the problem.

Like all growing things, plants need nutrients—18 essential nutrients, many of which are supplied by organic matter in the soil. Three nutrients, however, are usually lacking, so you need to add them every year or so for plants to grow well. That's why these are the three included in most fertilizers: nitrogen (N), phosphorous (P), and potassium (K). When you see a fertilizer bag marked 10-5-10, for example, that means it has 10 percent nitrogen, 5 percent phosphorus, and 10 percent potassium. (The rest is inert filler that makes spreading easier.)

There are two kinds of fertilizers to choose from: synthetic ones made from inorganic compounds and organic ones made from natural minerals, plant by-products, or animal matter. One big difference between the two is how long they take to work. Organic fertilizers are less concentrated and release nutrients more slowly. Synthetic formulas release nutrients quickly, but they don't last as long. Note: Because they are stronger (have higher N-P-K numbers), they can burn plants if not used as directed. You will probably pay more for slow-release synthetic fertilizer, but there's little chance of damage.

 TROUBLE • Discolored leaves? This may be caused by nutrient imbalance or deficiency or by soil that's too acid or alkaline. To rule out plant disease, take a few unhealthy leaves to your local nursery for diagnosis.

• Neighbors say the local soil is deficient in certain nutrients? To identify nutrient imbalance and get instructions on how to fix it, you'll need a professional soil test. Contact your local Cooperative Extension Service or a private lab in your area.

• Poor drainage? Beware: bad drainage can cause the same symptoms as missing nutrients. Try the easy soil tests on page 33 to check drainage. Correct it by adding organic matter (see page 32).

WHEN TO FERTILIZE?

Natural minerals, such as limestone, take a while to dissolve; these should be applied in fall so plants can use them next spring. Standard fertilizers (the 5-10-5 type) should be added in early spring, as soon as plants start to grow. Fertilize a growing plant by sprinkling dry fertilizer in a ring around it (called "side-dressing") or mixing liquid fertilizer with water and feeding while you water.

Use an inexpensive soil test kit to determine your soil pH. Take teaspoon samples from four different parts of your yard and mix to get a good cross-section. Do separate tests for the lawn and garden.

Pine bark mulch is cheap, easy, attractive, and nutritious. Nurseries sell it in bags.

SOIL-TEST RESOURCES

A&L Eastern Agricultural Labs Inc..... 804-743-9401

Luster Leaf Products, Inc....... 815-337-5560

Woods End Research Laboratory 207-293-2457

FERTILIZER SOURCES

Beaty Fertilizer Co., Inc. 800-845-2325

Earthgro 800-736-7645

Easy Gardener 800-327-9462

The Scotts Company........ 800-543-TURF

DRAINAGE

Persistent drainage problems may call for installation of drainage pipes that gather water and connect to a storm drain or catch basin.

Water moves from high ground to low. To have good drainage, you need to have positive grade —that's where the soil is highest at the foundation of the house and slopes away from the house into the yard. Negative grade is the opposite: the soil level by the foundation is lower than the rest of the yard. Negative grade can result in flooded basements when it rains.

When a new house "settles," you can get negative grade because the air pockets in the soil gradually work their way out, causing the soil level to drop. That's why the soil in the yard must be compacted, or pressed down to remove air pockets, before building a house.

How to fix drainage problems? Your choices are simple: 1) Dig a swale, or shallow trench, in the yard to capture the water and move it to another part of the yard; 2) install a dry well or underground pit filled with gravel that draws in water and percolates it through the ground; 3) carve out a catch basin, like a dry well but linked to your town's or city's underground drainage system; or 4) dig a trench and put down a perforated plastic pipe that carries water to a dry well or catch basin. All four of these solutions are best left to a landscape contractor (see page 22), as they won't work unless installed properly.

Every element in your yard, including the planting beds, walkways, and patios, must be properly graded (or pitched) to shed water.

TROUBLE • Water in the basement? It may be that you have negative grade around the foundation perimeter. Call a landscape contractor for an evaluation.

• Little puddles in the lawn after it rains? If they are shallow, fix them by putting down ½" of topsoil or compost and raking it between grass blades. Repeat until gone. For deeper puddles, remove the puddle-soaked sod and add enough topsoil or compost to make the soil level, replace sod, and water well.

ROUGH WORK

CHECKLIST ✔ Before any digging or excavating is done in your yard, locate all the electric, gas, and water lines. If they are not on your home survey, call your local utility companies and ask them where their lines are located on your property.

✔ Rough grading requires the use of heavy machinery, such as a skid-steer loader or push-blade bulldozer. Hire a landscape contractor to grade (or regrade) your yard.

✔ Slope is important for proper drainage. Allow at least 1" of slope for every 8' so that water can drain naturally.

If you must have drainage ditches in your yard, work them into the landscape by filling them with river stone, gravel, pebbles, or even beach glass.

DRAINAGE-SYSTEM RESOURCES

Advanced Drainage
Systems Inc......... 800-821-6710

Lester's Material
Service Inc. 847-223-7000

Soleno SPD Inc. 800-363-1471

WEED/PEST CONTROL

A few dandelions may be dandy, but if weeds start to overwhelm your yard, consider herbicides. Broadleaf herbicides are designed for lawns because they kill everything except grasses. Nonselective types kill grasses as well as broad-leaved weeds. Preemergent herbicides stop seeds from sprouting but don't affect existing weeds.

Eventually, something will bug your garden—weeds or leaf chompers or some disease. The strategies for all these troubles are basically the same.

First, identify the problem. Check under leaves and near branch tips for bugs. If holes in leaves appear overnight, look for shiny trails—sure signs of slugs or snails that hide during the day. Fine webs are signs of minute spider mites. Take sick-looking leaves or unknown bugs to a garden center or Cooperative Extension Service for identification.

Next, identify possible solutions. If you opt for chemicals, remember that herbicides kill only weeds and won't do a thing to stop bugs. Insecticides kill only bugs and won't help you fight diseases. Fungicides only control diseases, and most work only for specific ones. Fungicides tend to be the most dangerous pesticides for humans, so to avoid unnecessary exposure, make sure the one you use will work for the disease in question. This is good advice for any chemical control. Always read the label to make sure a product will do the job you want, and follow directions to avoid harming plants instead of helping them.

Check out some of the new pest-control products. Herbicidal soaps in squirt bottles are great for spot-treating individual weeds. Insecticidal soaps work for many small insects and are safe to use on most plants. Horticultural oil contains no poisons and works by smothering insects. Avoid using it or any other sprays on hot, sunny days, to minimize stress to plants, or on windy days, when sprays could blow back on you.

HOME REMEDIES

WEEDS:

• Dig out weeds before they form seeds.

• Pour boiling water on weeds in gravel paths or driveways.

• Mulch exposed soil to block weeds from sprouting (any that do sprout will be easy to pull because mulch keeps soil loose).

DISEASES:

• Take steps to improve air circulation so leaves dry quickly: 1) Prune over-hanging branches; 2) space plants far-ther apart; and 3) divide crowded perennials.

• Remove and destroy badly diseased leaves, branches, or entire plants. Clean up gardens in fall rather than spring.

• Make your own spray to control rust fungi, powdery mildew, and leaf-spot diseases. Dissolve 1 Tbsp. baking soda in 1 gal. water; add 1 Tbsp. vegetable oil and several drops of dishwashing liquid to help it stick. Spray on leaves every two weeks, as needed.

INSECTS:

• Pick off bugs if they're big. Drop bugs like beetles into soapy water; they'll drown overnight.

• Hose off small bugs. Repeat every few days until pests are gone.

• Sink margarine tubs into soil and fill with stale beer to trap slugs and snails. Or set out empty, upside-down grape-fruit halves at night to attract these critters; discard in the morning.

Powdery mildew afflicts a number of common garden plants, including bee balm (above). Symptoms are patches on leaves that look white to light gray and like flour (right). Control with fungicidal soap or the spray described in "Home Remedies," at left.

Ladybugs eat aphids (greenish, above) and other small insects that harm plants. Buying ladybugs is a waste of money; they just fly away when they are released. Encourage native ladybugs—which stick around long enough to help—by not using insecticides.

WEED/PEST-CONTROL SOURCES

AgrEvo Environmental
Health 800-438-5837

Bonide
Products, Inc. 800-536-8231

Gardens Alive! 812-537-8651

Ortho Books 800-225-2883

Safer, Inc. 612-703-4570

The Scotts
Company 800-543-TURF

LAWNS

Is the grass greener on the other side? It doesn't have to be. Read on and learn the easy art of growing and taking care of the lawn.

SMART GUIDE....................................42/43

NEW LAWNS 44/45

EXISTING LAWNS 46/47

LAWN MAINTENANCE 48/49

WATERING 50/51

MOWERS/TRIMMERS.......................52/53

PROBLEM LAWN/TOOLS..................54/55

LAWNS

To get lawn smart, use this easy number guide to identify and name all various plant parts and machines involved in taking care of a lawn. Detailed explanations of each item follow:

LAWN

1 . . . GRASS SEED

2 . . . CLEAN STRAW

3 . . . NEW GRASS

4 . . . ROOTS

5 . . . MATURE LAWN

6 . . . THATCH

7 . . . AERATION HOLES

8 . . . SHADED GRASS

9 . . . EARTHWORM

10 . . . EARTHWORM BURROW

11 . . . TREE TRUNK

12 . . . TREE ROOTS

WEEDS

13 . . . DANDELION

14 . . . SEED HEAD

15 . . . TAPROOT

16 . . . CRABGRASS

17 . . . CRABGRASS ROOTS

IRRIGATION SYSTEM

18 . . . IRRIGATION PIPE

19 . . . T CONNECTOR

20 . . . SPRINKLER HEAD

21 . . . WATERING DEPTH (6")

MOWERS

22 . . . REEL MOWER

23 . . . CUTTING BLADES

24 . . . POWER MOWER (rotary)

25 . . . CUTTING BLADES (rotary)

26 . . . BLADE HEIGHT ADJUSTMENT

27 . . . GRASS CLIPPINGS

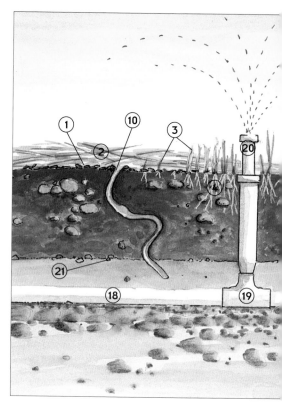

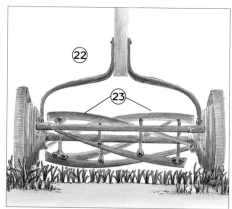

NEW LAWNS

Here piles of sod are ready to be put in place. In northern climates, put down sod or seed in late summer—cool fall weather encourages rapid establishment. In the South, late spring and early summer are the best times to start.

Lawns like the same soil as most plants: fertile, not too acidic or alkaline (see page 34), rich in organic matter, and not compacted (that means packed down by feet or wheels).

Whether it's raw land or dead lawn you're looking at, check first to see if it needs grading (see page 36) so that the soil drains properly. Next, consider how you will water it. An irrigation system (see page 51) is easier and less expensive to install *before* the lawn is in. Hire an irrigation contractor to plan out a system and lay the pipes. Finally, before seeding or sodding, the soil has to be cleared of weeds and raked.

To seed or to sod? What's the difference? Seeding involves scattering loose seeds on soil. It will take about six weeks for them to fill in. Laying down sod involves placing strips of full-grown grass (18" wide x 6' long) complete with its roots over soil. Sod is more expensive, but you get an instant lawn. Both require the same amount of watering.

Important note: To increase your lawn's ability to cope with disease, drought, and extreme heat and cold, use a mix of grasses. Seeding offers the most options for using a variety, since not all grasses or grass mixes are available in the form of sod.

GRASS CHOICES

Here is a listing of the pros and cons of lawn favorites. You can buy either a single type or a mix.

To seed 1,000 sq. ft., you'll need anywhere from 2 to 7 lbs. of seed, depending on the variety. Don't mow until your new grass reaches a height of 2" to 3".

🍂 🍂 BERMUDA GRASS—Pro: Spreads quickly; heat-, drought-, and salt-tolerant. Con: Poor shade tolerance; turns brown in winter.

🍂 🍂 🍂 FINE FESCUE—Pro: Shade- and drought-tolerant; needs little fertilizer. Con: Not good for wet sites.

🍂 🍂 KENTUCKY BLUEGRASS—Pro: Versatile; attractive; many varieties. Con: High-maintenance; poor drought and shade tolerance.

🍂 🍂 PERENNIAL RYEGRASS—Pro: Seeds germinate quickly; good wear tolerance. Con: Stops growing earlier in colder areas.

🍂 ST. AUGUSTINE—Pro: Grows quickly; shade-tolerant. Con: Low resistance to cold, disease, and bugs.

🍂 ZOYSIA GRASS—Pro: Dense growth; crowds out weeds; drought-tolerant. Con: Slow-grower; turns brown in winter.

 PREPARATION

 ✔ Check out the sun exposure in the yard. Spend a sunny day outdoors and observe how much sun the area gets. Does it receive full sun or only patches? Is any area shaded by trees?

✔ Test the soil (see page 34). If it's acidic, you'll need limestone; if it's alkaline, sulfur. Add according to manufacturer's instructions.

✔ Find out whether you have compacted soil: push a screwdriver into the ground, up to its handle. If you can't do this easily, your soil is compacted. Fix this by rototilling (turning over 4" of soil). You can rent rototillers.

✔ Put down 4" to 6" of good topsoil.

✔ Mix or roll seed into the top ¼" of soil. Cover with clean salt hay to contain moisture and keep birds from stealing the seed. Water daily for 15 minutes (see page 50).

TROUBLE

• Seed failed to sprout? 1) Could be you got old seeds. (Buy seeds marked for the current year.) 2) Lack of moisture. Newly seeded lawns need regular watering (turn on the sprinkler for 15 minutes each night) to keep the soil evenly moist. Once seedlings appear, gradually reduce watering, but never allow seedlings to wilt. After the first or second mowing, switch to normal watering patterns for your area (see page 50).

• Sod turned brown shortly after installation? Sod needs as much water as seeded lawn does until the roots have grown into the underlying soil. If increased watering does not restore the green in two to three weeks, replace the browned sod. (Sod is usually guaranteed against disease.)

• Gaps between strips of sod? This means that they weren't tightly fitted together. Purchase another strip of sod and cut it into thin strips, to fit into the gaps. Water these well until roots take hold.

LAWN SOURCES

Great Western Seed 541-928-3100

Lofts Seed, Inc. 888-77-LOFTS

Pennington Seed, Inc. 800-285-SEED

The Scotts Company 800-543-TURF

Turfgrass Producers, International 800-405-TURF

EXISTING LAWNS

For shady areas in northern climates, use varieties of Kentucky bluegrass developed for shade, such as 'Bristol', 'Benson', 'Birka', 'Eclipse', 'Glade', and 'Nugget'.

Existing lawns are like old carpets: eventually, they'll begin to show wear and tear. Drought, disease, insects, or too many ball games in the same area will result in bare or weedy spots—signs of a deteriorating lawn.

If your lawn deterioration isn't too severe (more than 50 percent of the area has good turf), then your renovation can be limited to overseeding. Don't panic— it's easy. Simply spread seeds over your whole area of lawn—damaged areas as well as healthy ones. Overseeding can upgrade the quality of your lawn because you can add improved varieties

of grass, ones that require less care and are disease- and drought-resistant.

If over half of your lawn area is in bad shape, plan on complete renovation. This means that weeds and the remaining grass will have to be killed. (Sorry, but it's all got to go.) You can accomplish this with a nonspecific weed killer (see page 38) or by using a rototiller (a machine that cuts into the soil and turns it over) to a depth of 2" to 3". Or you can hire a lawn contractor to bring in a machine that cuts grooves in the ground and at the same time deposits grass seed into the grooves.

STEPS IN OVERSEEDING

✔First correct the causes of deterioration. 1) Test soil to determine soil pH and nutrient levels (see page 34). 2) If soil is compacted, aerate lawn (see page 55). 3) If puddles last a long time after rain, fix poor drainage problems by grading (see page 36). 4) In shady spots, remove lower tree limbs to let in more light.

✔Dig up weeds or zap them with a weed killer. Check the label of the weed killer first; it may prevent grass seed from sprouting unless you wait a specified period of time.

✔Prior to overseeding, cut the lawn short—to about 1". Rake well to remove clippings and grass debris on top of the soil so that seeds can more easily reach the soil. Water area well.

✔For a small lawn, scatter seeds by hand. For large lawns, use a spreader (see page 55).

✔Water newly seeded areas 15 minutes a day in early morning or in late afternoon. Do this until grass seedlings are visible, in about two to three weeks.

 TROUBLE •Shady property? Select blends of shade-tolerant grasses, such as fine fescue; St. Augustine works well in southern regions. Keep grass on the long side. Don't overdo it with fertilizer or watering.

Choose extra tough grasses that withstand the abuse that play areas get. Best bets are Bermuda grass, zoysia, tall fescue (a fine fescue), and perennial ryegrass.

LAWN MAINTENANCE

Actually, a hay field more accurately represents the natural growth habit of your lawn. Ergo, getting it under control requires active maintenance.

Mowing is one of the most important parts of lawn care. Some rules: 1) Mow frequently because cutting more than one-third of the height of the grass blades at once actually stresses the grass. 2) In cool regions cut grass shorter in spring and fall and longer in summer. In warm regions mow shorter in summer and longer in spring and fall. 3) Leave short clippings on the lawn. As they decay, they return valuable nutrients to the soil. Longer clippings should be raked up. 4) Cut grass in straight lines. 5) Avoid mowing when grass is wet.

Now about fertilizing. Yes, it's a good idea. Experts recommend fertilizing a lawn twice a year—in spring and fall. Fertilizing in spring greens up the grass, (see page 34–35). Use a lawn fertilizer marked 30-4-4 for this. The fall application helps the grass better survive winter. Use one marked 10-18-20 then. Apply with a spreader (see page 55).

Hard, packed-down soil is one of the main causes of lawn problems. Loosen up the soil by taking out finger-size plugs of soil with either a manual or a mechanical aeration device (see page 55). These small holes will allow fertilizer and water to better reach the roots.

Using a mix of different grass types, such as varieties of Kentucky bluegrass (shown here), will keep your lawn looking better than a single variety of seed.

MOW BETTER

Before you mow, check the height setting on mower and adjust to accommodate both the season and the type of grass you have. If you have the following grasses, cut:

Bermuda grass and zoysia very short—1" in summer, 1½" in spring/fall.

St. Augustine medium to high—2" in summer in the South, 3" in summer in the West, 2" in spring/fall in all regions.

Fine fescue, Kentucky bluegrass, and perennial ryegrass medium to high—2½" to 3" in summer, 2" in spring/fall.

TROUBLE • Patches of grass over slight elevations turning brown? Lawn mowers (especially wide ones) cut closely or even scalp bumps in the yard. During dry periods, this low-cut grass will turn brown. Correct by slicing off sod, scraping away some soil (or, if it's a dip, adding soil), and replanting the sod.

• Thatch buildup? Thatch is the old, dead grass that can suffocate your lawn. Use a thatch rake (see page 55) to remove it.

• Dog poop? Dog droppings will first create brown spots in a lawn, then hyper-green ones. To avoid problems, remove and discard it (do not compost, as it may carry disease).

If you have a high-traffic area (in this case, a driveway) and want it green, plant zoysia grass or fine fescue between cobbles or stepping-stones. You still need to mow, water, and fertilize, as you would any lawn.

WATERING

When to water? Watering during midday wastes water because much is lost to evaporation. You can save a lot by running sprinkler hoses in the cooler morning or early evening. Generally, lawns require 1½" of water every two weeks; sandy soils need this amount every week.

Most of us do more harm than good when we water. So pay attention; becoming water wise can save money, prevent waste of a valuable natural resource, and make your grass healthy—all at the same time.

First, figure out the texture of your soil. Hold a clump of moist soil in your hand. If it sticks together and you can actually roll it into a ball, it is clay. Clay soil holds more water than sandy soil, so you need to apply more water at one time but less frequently. If your soil falls apart easily in your hands, even when moist, it is sandy. Sandy soil can't store much water, so it needs more frequent watering than clay soil (see page 32).

Next, you'll want to be sure that, after watering, the water has penetrated 6" deep into the soil. (Use a screwdriver to create a hole and push a wooden Popsicle stick into it; after a minute, the stick should be entirely damp.) Keep watering until the top 6" is moist. If water starts running off, stop and let it soak in for an hour before continuing. Watering to the appropriate depth makes grass more drought-resistant by encouraging deep roots that can reach far for water. Shallow watering produces shallow roots that dry out quickly.

How often to water? When footprints become visible in the lawn, it's time to water. What to water with? You have three basic choices: 1) a sprinkler hose (a hose with holes), 2) a hose with a sprinkler attachment, or 3) an irrigation system. Note: Irrigation systems water by schedules you set.

IRRIGATION SYSTEMS

Selecting an irrigation system can be a little complicated, so it's best to start by hiring a lawn contractor with irrigation-design experience to help you design, install, and calibrate a system for your yard.

Irrigation systems include control systems, valves, rain gauges, pumps, underground piping, sprinklers, and, often, timers. While the components of any system are basically the same, the type and quality will vary. Insist on getting updated elements. The latest solid-state control systems, for example, have fewer problems than earlier systems.

Install separate zones to accommodate the watering needs of different sections of lawn. Grass in shade needs less water, for instance, than grass in full sun.

To set the timer for your system (or for a sprinkler), check the clock and water until the top 6" of soil is wet. Check the clock again and set the timer to water for that length of time during future waterings.

Pop-up sprinkler heads can rise up 4" to 12" above the ground and can spray up to a full 360°. When watering is completed, heads retract into the ground.

SHORTCUTS • When you want or need to conserve water, choose grasses that need little water. For Northern regions: red fescue, chewings fescue, and hard fescue. For warm Southern regions: hybrid Bermuda. In high elevations: blue grama, or buffalo grass.

TROUBLE • Areas of brown grass? The problem is probably uneven watering. Be sure to cover the entire lawn as you move a sprinkler around. If you have an irrigation system, have it reevaluated to check for poor placement of sprinkler heads or water pressure that is too high or too low for the system.

• Broken irrigation pipes? Failure to drain irrigation pipes before winter in cold climates can cause pipes to rupture. Have new pipes installed below freezing depth and drain them before cold weather arrives.

• Sprinkler system broken and you have to water by hand? Buy a $4 sprayer and attach it to the end of your hose. Mentally divide your lawn up into 10-yd. squares and water each square. Spray each section until the soil is moist to a depth of 6" (be patient—it takes a while).

SPRINKLER SOURCES

A. M. Andrews 503-244-1163

L. R. Nelson
Corporation 800-NELSON8

Naan Sprinklers &
Irrigation Systems . . 714-903-8181

Seasons Irrigation
Supply 800-396-0100

Submatic Irrigation
Systems 800-692-4100

MOWERS AND TRIMMERS

OPERATOR PRESENCE CONTROL
shuts off engine when released, reducing the chance of injury if the operator slips or trips

WHEEL SPEED CONTROL
provides forward self-propulsion, making the chore of pushing the mower up hills or slopes considerably easier

ENGINE THROTTLE CONTROL
regulates the speed of the engine

ROTARY MOWER

STARTER CORD
is pulled to start mower

OIL CAP
is removed to add new oil, once a season

COLLECTION BAG
collects grass clippings for disposal or composting

CUTTING DECK WIDTH
determines how wide the mower will cut in one pass

DECK HEIGHT ADJUSTER
lets you raise or lower the deck to change the cutting height for varying grass seasons or conditions

It's pretty simple—mowers fall into two basic types: reel and rotary. Reel mowers use a scissors-type action to leave a very neat cut. Choose from 14"-wide models to 20". You can also get them with motors—alas, at a much higher price.

A rotary mower has a single rotating blade powered by a small engine that slices grass. The cutting height of a rotary mower can be set higher than with reel mowers, so they're good for all grass types. Rotaries come in standard 18" to 23" widths and then in wide cuts, from 36" to 72", for extralarge lawns.

Choose rotary mowers by model and engine type. Walk-behind models are good for level, small to medium lawns. Riding models (aka lawn tractors) are great for large lawns. (Both can come with bags to collect lawn clippings as you mow.) Electric engines are quiet and ideal for small yards. (The cord only reaches so far.) Gas engines cover more ground but require more maintenance.

Now for something completely new: mulching lawn mowers. These babies have a unique blade that not only cuts grass but also pulverizes clippings. No need for a collection bag; no more raking up clippings. Best of all, it creates instant mulching for your lawn.

Trimmers are long shafts with an engine and a rapidly rotating nylon string that trims grass where the lawn mower can't reach: lawn edges, around fences, or on steep slopes. Electric trimmers are light but require an extension cord. Gas models are heavier and easily cut tall, tougher weeds and grass.

The nylon string used on trimmers comes in various thicknesses. Thicker nylon is best for cutting tough weeds. Thin nylon is fine for long grass that does not have many weeds.

 ## SELECTING MOWERS/TRIMMERS

✔ Reel mowers are best for level lawns without a lot of weeds. Rotary mowers offer more cutting strength for weeds, have adjustable cutting heights, and require less effort to maneuver on hills and slopes.

✔ Engine sizes range from 2 to 8 hp (horsepower) for walk-behinds and up to 14 hp for riding mowers. The small engines found on lightweight mowers make these easier to push around. Mowers with larger engines (5 or 5.5 hp and up) are heavier but more durable than those with smaller engines.

✔ Narrower (18"- to 23"-wide) mowers are easier to maneuver in tight spaces. Mowers with wide cutting decks (24" and wider) reduce the number of passes you have to make and therefore cut your mowing time, but they are best on level lawns.

✔ For the greatest versatility, get a multipurpose trimmer. You can get accessory heads with blades instead of nylon string for tough weeds, sawlike blades for cutting brush, and heads that function as edgers. The last are great for maintaining a neat edge between lawns and flower beds.

✔ Gas trimmers have two-cycle engines that run on a mix of gas and two-cycle oil. The owner's manual will tell you the exact mix. Fuel won't last longer than 30 days before going flat.

 • Mower or trimmer won't start? It may be due to old fuel, fouled spark plug, or dirty air filter. Don't use fuel that's been stored for more than 30 days. Remove the spark plug and check for buildup of carbon at the tip. Regularly remove and clean the air filter.

• Grass blades looking ragged? Time to sharpen your reel or rotary mower blade. Remove mower blade and bring it to a store that sells lawn mowers; many will sharpen blades for a minimal charge.

• Excessive vibration in the mower or trimmer? Something is loose. Check and tighten all bolts and fasteners on the outside frame. Or you may have damaged the blade going over too many rocks. Check and replace, if necessary.

• Injuring trees with your mower? Create a grass-free zone around them: plant a bed of ground cover or apply a layer of mulch (wood chips) around it.

SELECTING A LAWN-CARE SERVICE

1) Ask for referrals from services most recent clients. 2) Get a list of services provided by the service. 3) Find out which ones are guaranteed. 4) Get proof of liability insurance. 5) Inquire about the employees who will be doing the job. Are they experienced? Are they certified to apply pesticides? 6) Get a written contract that specifies exact services and fees. 7) Inspect the work. Be on the alert, for instance, for trampled flower beds or injury to the base of trees caused by careless lawn mower jockeys.

MOWER-AND-TRIMMER SOURCES

American Lawn
Mower Company. . . 800-633-1501

Black &
Decker 800-54-HOWTO

John Deere. 800-537-8233

Lawn-Boy 800-LBMOWER

Toro 800-348-2424

Troy-Bilt 800-828-5500

THE PROBLEM LAWN

Frequent, shallow watering, mowing grass too short, or overuse of fertilizers can make grass more susceptible to disease.

Got an Addams family lawn complete with weeds and insects? For a quick fix, use chemical pesticides, which include herbicides (these kill weeds) and insecticides (these kill insects). See page 38 for more information. Weed killer can be applied anytime weeds are actively growing, but avoid applying it in windy or hot weather to avoid injury to you, grass, or nearby plants. Be patient! It will take several days or weeks for weeds to die. Use insecticides that are aimed at controlling the specific insect pests in your lawn. (This means you'll have to find out which of the buggers are causing problems.) Most pests will be killed within hours or a few days.

While chemical pesticides are effective, the truth is they do not discriminate. They may kill the many beneficial creatures in the soil and lawn. Many of these, whether insects, bacteria, or fungi (yes, you should learn about them), provide natural defenses against lawn pests and diseases. You may have to accept a few weeds and thin spots. Choose organic products when you think it appropriate.

PEST-CONTROL RESOURCES

CHEMICAL

AgrEvo Environmental Health 800-438-5837

Pennington Seed, Inc. 800-285-SEED

The Scotts Company. 800-543-TURF

ORGANIC

Gardens Alive! 812-537-8651

Peaceful Valley Farm Supply Co. 530-272-4769

Ringer Corp. 612-703-4570

LAWN TOOLS

To keep your lawn from becoming a problem lawn, you'll need something besides a mower and a sprinkler. Here are the basic hand and power tools you'll need.

THINGS TO BUY

CHECKLIST ✔ Spreader: Get these for annual fertilizing, seeding new lawns, overseeding, and spreading forms of herbicides or pesticides. Handheld models are handy but good only for small areas; they won't give you even coverage. Push models are best for multiple uses. Get one with a plastic bucket (called a hopper) that won't rust. (Hose out after applying lawn chemicals.)

✔ Thatch rake: If you've got over ½" of thatch (the dead, strawlike stuff at the base of the grass blade), you need to rake it off, usually once a year or so. (If you have less, you can leave it.) The rake's short tines are designed to get right to the thatch. Models with wheels make the job easier.

✔ Lawn rake: To prevent leaves from smothering lawn rake fallen leaves with a large bamboo, plastic, or metal rake.

✔ Aerator: Aerating lawns keeps grass healthy by counteracting soil compaction and helping water and air reach roots. Consider renting one; you'll only need it once a year. Aerate anytime your soil isn't wet; it's especially good right before you fertilize. Core aerators, machines that remove slender plugs of soil, do the best job. To aerate while you mow, strap on a pair of aerator sandals.

✔ Edger: Your grass may creep into flower beds or over driveways. Stop it with an edger. Manual edgers are just sharp blades with long handles; stomping on the top edge neatly slices the grass. If you have lots to do, you may want a power edger, which uses a gas or electric engine to drive a toothed, circular blade.

✔ Weeder: Despite your best efforts, weeds will pop up here and there. You can spot-treat with a squirt bottle of herbicide, but it's almost as easy to dig them out. Weeders come in many shapes and sizes. Dandelion forks—long, straight blades with toothed ends—get deep roots out. The curved part of this weeder (below) helps you pop out shallow weeds.

Self-propelled core aerator

Spreader

Power edger

Dandelion fork

Thatch rake with wheels

Aerator sandals

GET YARD SMART

GROUND COVERS

If lawn maintenance is low on your list of fun things to do, put down a carefree carpet of ground cover. Better still, these hardy plants resist bugs and pests and don't need fertilizer. Discover how easy they are.

GROUND COVER NURSERY SOURCES

Bluestone Perennials	800-852-5243
Carroll Gardens Inc.	800-638-6334
Milaegar's Inc.	414-639-2040
Peekskill Nurseries	914-245-5595
Savory's Gardens	612-941-8755
Spring Hill Nurseries	800-582-8527
Wayside Gardens	800-845-1124
White Flower Farm	800-503-9624

SMART GUIDE....................................58/59

SUNNY GROUND COVERS...............60/61

SHADY GROUND COVERS 62/63

ORNAMENTAL GRASSES 64/65

GROUND COVERS

To get ground-cover smart, use this easy number guide to plant and care for your ground cover. Detailed explanations of each item follow in this chapter.

PREPARING FOR PLANTING

1 . . . PREPARE BARE SOIL (remove grass and other vegetation from planting area)

2 . . . MIX COMPOST INTO SOIL (not shown)

3 . . . DIG PLANTING HOLES AS LARGE AS ROOTS

4 . . . SPACE HOLES 12" APART AND STAGGER (plants will fill out in a few months)

5 . . . NEW PLANTS (sold in flats)

PLANTING

6 . . . PLACE PLANTS IN HOLES AND FILL WITH SOIL

7 . . . WATER WELL (not shown)

8 . . . COVER SOIL WITH MULCH

CARING FOR GROUND COVER

9 . . . TRIM ALONG WALKWAY

10 . . . CUTTINGS MAY BE TRANSPLANTED ELSEWHERE (not shown)

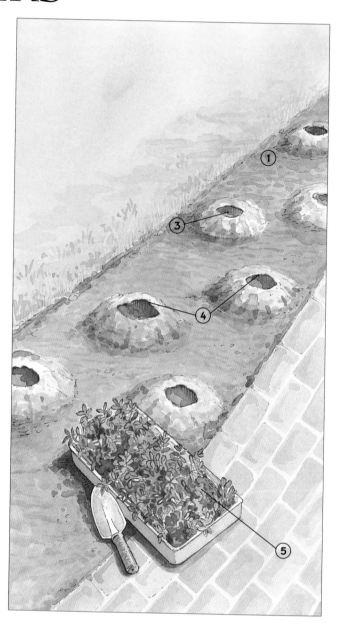

SUNNY GROUND COVERS

Some ground covers are hardy enough to withstand light to moderate foot traffic, like these two varieties of creeping thyme. Planted in pathways located in sunny areas, they will release a spicy fragrance when walked upon. Very nice.

Great news for those who are yard-challenged: ground covers give new meaning to the idea of low-maintenance. They require no mowing, trimming, or pruning, and most are so hardy they resist drought, diseases, and pests, so they save on water, pesticides, and fertilizers. In plant-land, that's pretty impressive. Plant them instead of a lawn or use them for problem spots, such as slopes that are too steep to mow. Best of all—they crowd out the weeds, so no weeding.

There is an abundance of sun-loving ground covers out there. To help you choose, consider some of the following. Some ground covers grow fast, some slow; some are tall, some short; some flower and some don't. Fast-growers like AJUGA grow so quickly (*vigorous* is the technical term) they can become invasive if not controlled. Corral these by surrounding the plants with edging (2"- to 3"-high plastic strips set into the ground). Slow-growers like JUNIPER are better-behaved, but take longer to cover the area. SEDUM, ICE PLANT, CREEPING THYME, and ajuga have colorful flowers, while EUONYMUS and juniper offer foliage that lasts in winter.

Trailing ice plants (above) bloom in vivid shades of red or pink from March to May. Ice plants also come in other bold colors. Creeping juniper (left) provides year-round color, from silvery to blue-green.

BUYING AND PLANTING

 CHECKLIST

✔ Consider height first. If ground cover will fill a small space, buy a shortie; if it will run along a fence, get a tall one.

✔ Evergreen ground covers provide a nice contrast to plants that fade in winter. Popular evergreen choices are euonymus and juniper.

✔ How much to buy? Measure the area you want to cover so your plant seller will know how much you need.

✔ Prepare the area before planting. Remove grass and weeds. Optional: spread a couple of inches of peat moss (see page 32) and mix it into soil to keep it moist.

✔ If you can't afford lots of plants, set them farther apart and spread 2" to 3" of mulch (wood chips or shredded bark) between to stop weeds.

PLANT SMART

PLANT	HEIGHT	ZONE
Ajuga	3"–10"	🍃 🍃 🍃
Creeping juniper	8"–24"	🍃 🍃 🍃
Creeping thyme	3"–6"	🍃 🍃 🍃
Euonymus	24"	🍃 🍃
Ice plant	6"–12"	🍃
Sedum	2"–8"	🍃 🍃 🍃 🍃

✔ To convert lawn to ground cover you have to first kill the lawn. When grass is growing and weather is warm, cover grass with black plastic sheets for two weeks. Then remove the plastic and rake up dead grass. Till the soil and plant the ground cover.

 TROUBLE

• Smothered ground cover? A carpet of wet tree leaves can smother a ground cover when plants emerge in spring. Clear ground cover of all debris in late fall or late winter.

• Weeds taking over freshly planted ground cover? Cover the area under the ground cover with several inches of mulch—shredded cedar or pine bark is a good choice because it allows ground cover to spread while keeping down weeds.

SHADY GROUND COVERS

This planting of pachysandra solves two problems: it covers a shady spot and tops a slope, which can be difficult to mow—especially along the wall's edge.

There's more to ground covers than the old evergreen standbys, IVY and PACHYSANDRA, which are often planted indiscriminately in any shady spot. Try adding a large-leaved HOSTA or a border of a dainty Hosta variety. Even the old standards don't have to be dark green; ivy and pachysandra come in silver-leaved and variegated (striped or spotted with a lighter color) varieties. Just a single silver or variegated plant will help head off visual monotony. Contrasting the bold texture of large hostas with the delicate SWEET WOODRUFF or the small leaves of PERIWINKLE (also known as VINCA) will help, too.

Like their sun-loving counterparts, shade-loving ground covers are easy to maintain and come in a variety of heights and growth habits.

Some even flower. While pachysandra flowers aren't too exciting, hosta, sweet woodruff, periwinkle, and LILY-OF-THE-VALLEY show off attractive flowers in late spring or summer. Lily-of-the-valley is particularly nice near a window or by a door because it's so fragrant. All are hardy and easy to grow, and they are wonderful antidotes to any dark, sad-looking corners of your yard. You can also liven things up by planting flowering annuals amid your ground cover.

CHECKLIST BUYING, PLANTING, AND CARE

✔Figure out the height and speed of growth you want.

✔Consider leaf and bloom color. For evergreens, go with periwinkle or pachysandra.

✔Before planting, the soil needs to be weeded, composted, and turned over (see page 58).

✔Because they have to share nutrients with the plants that are shading them, give shady ground covers frequent light sprinklings of fertilizer from spring to early summer.

 SHORTCUTS •Plant pachysandras and hostas in the dark shade of particularly dense trees.

•Under deciduous trees (those that lose their leaves), pair shade-loving ground covers with daffodils, crocuses, and snowdrops (see page 114). These bulbs bloom before the trees leaf in spring, while the ground cover hides their fading leaves in summer.

 **TROUBLE** •Ground covers scraggly over tree roots? Trees hog water and nutrients, leaving little for the ground covers. During dry spells, soak every few days. Annual doses of a standard garden fertilizer help ground covers compete with tree roots.

•Holes in your hosta leaves? Slugs like to feast on hostas. Set dishes of cheap beer into the ground to trap and drown these pests or use commercial slug bait traps, available at local garden centers.

In this shady garden there is a mixture of height and texture: 1) a variegated hosta, 2) the single-color 'Royal Standard' hosta, 3) ostrich ferns, and 4) winter creeper euonymus.

PLANT SMART

PLANT	HEIGHT	ZONE
Hosta	6"–36"	🍃 🍃 🍃
Ivy	6"–12"	🍃 🍃
Lily-of-the-valley	6"–12"	🍃 🍃 🍃
Pachysandra	8"–12"	🍃 🍃
Periwinkle (Vinca)	6"–10"	🍃 🍃
Sweet woodruff	6"–12"	🍃 🍃

POISON IVY

Look out for vines with shiny green leaves in threes.

Poison ivy is not the ivy to use as a ground cover; handle this bad boy with care because every part of it causes an itchy rash. Even the smoke from burning it can be an irritant to the lungs and eyes. To eliminate it from your property, use a nonresidual, systemic herbicide spray (see page 38.) If the poison ivy is twining high up around tree trunks or fence posts, cut the vine as high up as you can and spray the bottom leaves to kill the plant. Note: Clean the blades of any tools used with rubbing alcohol because the plant's oil can remain active for months and can still inflame your skin if you touch it.

ORNAMENTAL GRASSES

Believe it or not, there are garden trends, and the latest one is ornamental grasses, so called because of their decorative foliage. These beauties make great, low-maintenance ground covers. They can be planted in masses to cover what you want to cover. Bonus: they can add great color, too. BLUE FESCUE adds a steely blue for three seasons of the year, and FOUNTAIN GRASS offers creamy flowers atop arching green clumps.

Some of the taller types, such as MAIDEN GRASS (3' to 6') and GIANT FEATHER GRASS (2' to 6'), can double as wonderful garden accents or even create a privacy border or hedge.

Good news: grasses are resistant to insects and other pests, need little watering, and are weed-free. Moreover, they can stand up to coastal winds. Most grasses prefer full sun and tolerate only light shade. More good news: don't use fertilizer; grasses don't like it.

Ornamental grasses typically grow in clumps that increase in circumference each year. A few, including RIBBON GRASS, don't clump but spread by means of underground horizontal stems called rhizomes. Rhizomatous varieties of ornamental grasses grow and spread the fastest; keep these guys in check by trimming them back before new growth in spring.

Ornamental grasses, such as 1) clumpy blue fescue, blend well with sun-loving ground covers like 2) low-spreading junipers, 3) geraniums, or 4) sedges.

Late fall brings golden color to many tall ornamental grasses, like these different varieties of maiden grass. Taller ground covers not only cover a lot of ground (if you have loads of space) but also are good for creating an informal border along the edge of paths, patios, and decks.

✔ Most grasses are sold one clump per container. You will have to mass several to cover any area. Space them out so there is enough room for them to grow to the size listed on the plant's tag.

✔ Water generously but infrequently to encourage roots to grow deeply. Deep roots mean greater resistance to drought.

✔ Trim most ornamental grasses in early spring. Cut plants completely to the ground—don't worry, you'll get vigorous spring growth.

SHORTCUTS • If you want to increase your stock of planted grasses, dig up a clump in early spring before new growth starts. You can cut or pull it apart into smaller root clumps. Replant immediately.

PLANT SMART

PLANT	HEIGHT	ZONE
Blue fescue	6"–12"	
Fountain grass	1½'–3'	
Giant feather grass	2'–6'	
Maiden grass	3'–6'	
Perennial quaking grass	1'–2'	
Ribbon grass	2'–5'	

CHECKLIST BUYING AND PLANTING

✔ Consider height first. They all grow fast, and some are towering.

✔ Color: Look for shades that will complement what you have in your yard. Know that the greenish summer colors will bleach to gold or tan in late fall and winter.

✔ Texture: some are feathery, some spiky.

✔ Weed and turn over the soil before planting. Add only slow-release fertilizer or peat moss (see pages 32–35) because the nitrogen in common fertilizers, which causes spurts of growth, will make plants floppy.

TREES

What's the first thing you notice in anyone's yard? Most likely, it's the trees. Whether you're planting a little one for the first time or managing a huge sugar maple, here are the inside tips to make them flourish. Read on and discover how.

SMART GUIDE 68/69

SHADE TREES 70/71

EVERGREENS 72/73

FLOWERING TREES 74/75

SPECIALTY TREES 76/77

FRUIT/NUT TREES 78/79

TREE NURSERY SOURCES

Green Glen Nursery 815-723-1140

Gurney's Seed & Nursery Co.. 605-665-1671

Miller Nurseries 800-836-9630

Musser Forests 800-643-8319

Savage Nursery 615-668-8902

Stark Bro's. 800-325-4180

TREES

To get tree smart, use this easy number guide to identify and name all the parts of your tree and learn how to plant and care for it. Detailed explanations of each item follow in this chapter.

PLANTING TREES

1 . . . DIG A HOLE AS DEEP AS ROOT BALL AND TWICE AS WIDE

2 . . . SLIDE OR LIFT TREE INTO HOLE

3 . . . UNTIE BURLAP

4 . . . FOLD BACK BURLAP (remove if synthetic)

5 . . . FILL HOLE WITH MIX OF PEAT MOSS AND SOIL

6 . . . WATER EVERY OTHER DAY THROUGH FIRST GROWING SEASON (not shown)

7 . . . COVER SOIL WITH MULCH

8 . . . INSERT STAKE FOR SUPPORT (until tree is established)

GROWING TREES

9 . . . TRUNK

10 . . . CANOPY (tree's perimeter)

11 . . . ROOT SYSTEM

12 . . . BRANCH

13 . . . LEAVES

14 . . . ROOTS GROW AT LEAST AS WIDE AS CANOPY

15 . . . MULCH ANNUALLY (not shown)

16 . . . PRUNE LIGHTLY IF NECESSARY, TO ACHIEVE GOOD SHAPE (not shown)

PRUNING TREES

17 . . . TRIM LOWER LIMBS BACK FOR GROUND CLEARANCE

18 . . . CUT AND REMOVE BROKEN OR DAMAGED LIMBS

19 . . . REMOVE CROSSING BRANCHES

20 . . . PRUNE UPPER BRANCHES TO LET LIGHT INTO CANOPY

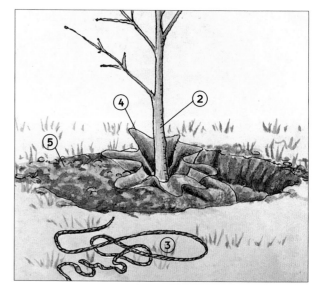

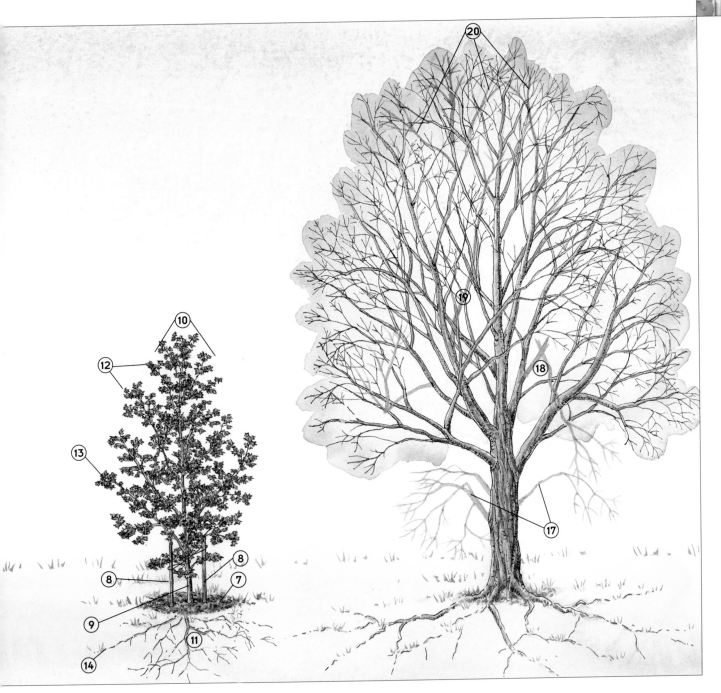

SHADE TREES

Large older trees like this sugar maple should be checked for such tree hazards as cracks in the trunk or major limbs, deadwood, and large limbs joined by tight, V-shaped forks—these are all signs of structural instability. Call in a tree service as soon as you notice a problem.

Like an air conditioner, a large, leafy tree can provide significant cooling during the heat of the day. Shade trees can also become a central focus in your yard because of their size and shape. And if these aren't enough reasons to plant a shade tree, real estate appraisers claim that large shade trees increase the resale value of most homes. You can't go wrong with SUGAR MAPLE, AMERICAN HORNBEAM, THORNLESS HONEYLOCUST, AMERICAN SWEETGUM, JAPANESE ZELKOVA, and SOUTHERN LIVE OAK.

When choosing trees for your yard, be aware of their ultimate height and width. Shade trees are lifetime investments. You don't want to be cutting one

down after 10 or 15 years because its limbs or roots are too close to the house, power lines, or septic tank. A sugar maple, for instance, eventually becomes huge and wide-spreading—up to 75' tall and 50' wide. That's great for large properties, but not for small yards. A smaller tree, such as American hornbeam, is a better choice for small properties.

What about falling leaves? Most shade trees are deciduous, meaning they shed their leaves in fall. If you have lots of shade trees, that means serious raking and gutter cleaning. Consider mixing in some evergreens.

SELECTION AND PLACEMENT

✔ Placement: you'll want to note the changing position of the sun throughout the day and the areas to be shaded, like portions of the house, a patio, or an outdoor play area.

✔ Slow-growing trees—sugar maples, American hornbeams, and Southern live oaks—last for generations. Fast-growing trees—poplar, red maple, and willow—have weak branches that may blow down in storms, and they tend to be short-lived.

✔ Choose trees that are resistant to pests or diseases, such as American sweetgum and Japanese zelkova—which looks a lot like, but is a lot more disease-resistant than, the stately old elms that were killed by elm disease.

✔ For instant shade (and big bucks), you can buy a large tree (10' to 15' high). Smaller trees (under 5') are less expensive, and you can plant them yourself.

Plant a tree like 1) thornless honeylocust because it casts a very light shade, so other plants can grow nearby. This garden features 2) rhododendrons, 3) begonias, 4) dahlias, and 5) phlox, which prefer mostly sunny spots.

• Lots of bare branches in your tree? 1) Check leaves for insects or disease. If you have a large tree, call in a licensed tree specialist to evaluate the tree's condition. 2) Check the soil. Try pushing a screwdriver into the ground; if it won't go in easily, compacted soil may be preventing the tree's roots from getting enough air and water. Aerate the lawn around the tree (see page 55) and spread a layer of compost (see page 32).

• Nothing growing under your tree? Many shade trees, because of the size of their leaves, won't allow enough sunlight through. Try shade-loving ground covers (see page 62) or fescue grass (see page 45).

• Leaves yellowing? 1) Soil acidity or a lack of nutrients could be starving your tree. Have your soil tested (see page 34). 2) Poor drainage (look for puddles). For new trees, dig up the tree, raise soil level by 6", and replant; for existing trees, install drainage pipes—piling on more dirt will only smother the roots.

• Old tree with long limbs? Call a licensed tree service to prune and, if need be, secure limbs with wire cable.

PLANT SMART

PLANT	HEIGHT	ZONE
American hornbeam	20'–30'	
American sweetgum	60'–75'	
Japanese zelkova	50'–80'	
Southern live oak	40'–80'	
Sugar maple	60'–75'	
Thornless honeylocust	30'–70'	

EVERGREENS

Yes, evergreen trees really do keep their leaves and their green color all year long. That's a big help when winter comes and the landscape is looking brown and gray. There are two kinds of evergreens: those with needle-shaped leaves and those with broad leaves. Needle-leaved guys, such as FIR, PINE, and SPRUCE, are very tolerant of the cold and make excellent windscreens. The broad-leaved varieties, such as HOLLY and YAUPON, are not so cold-hardy; they're better for shrub borders and foundation planting.

Use evergreens to frame views or to create a solid dark background to show off flower gardens or small flowering trees. Bonus: they can add interest to winter landscapes by providing shelter for birds and other wildlife.

On a more practical level, evergreens can be used to create boundaries or to act as privacy screens and noise reducers. When planted as a windbreak along the northern and western borders of a property, they can help reduce home heating costs.

Because pines, spruces, and firs can get to be very large trees, plant them at a distance from the house. If put next to the house, they'll block windows, create excessive shade, and promote moisture problems for the house (because of a lack of air circulation).

A simple landscape design trick: plant related evergreens of different sizes, shapes, and colors (but that require similar care). This garden features 1) Norway spruce, 2) Colorado blue spruce, 3) 'Montgomery' dwarf blue spruce, 4) blue-needled white fir, 5) dwarf Alberta spruce, and, on the ground, 6) varieties of Scotch heather for color.

PLANTING A CHRISTMAS TREE

Why buy a cut tree when you could have a live tree at Christmas and then plant it in your yard? Here's how: 1) Order your live tree from a local nursery and ask for December 21 delivery. 2) Dig a planting hole (see page 68). If your ground will freeze, do so in early winter and store soil where it will not freeze. 3) Cover the hole with boards, to keep out the elements. 4) Once tree arrives, water frequently and decorate. 5) After one week indoors, plant tree in the hole and fill in with the soil previously set aside. 6) Water until soil is thoroughly moist but not soggy.

 PLANTING AND CARE

CHECKLIST

✔ For planting instructions, see Smart Guide, page 68.

✔ After planting, water well (until all water is absorbed). Large trees may need staking before watering. For all but sandy soils, a deep watering once a week will do (sandy soil needs more).

✔ Mulch with a 3"- to 4"-deep layer of pine needles, shredded wood chips, compost (see page 32), or pine bark "nuggets" around plants. Leave a couple of inches of breathing room around the stem or trunk.

✔ Fertilize at planting with tree food recommended by your nursery, then annually in early spring. To fertilize established trees, use a crowbar to punch about a dozen holes 12" deep. Arrange holes in a random pattern beneath the spread of the branches—not too close to the trunk, to avoid damaging major roots. Pour in tree food, then fill the holes with soil.

Evergreens come in all sizes and shapes—tall and narrow, conical, or rounded. This red pine can reach 50' to 80' high and half as wide.

 TROUBLE

• Needles or leaves dropping? Even evergreens shed old leaves or needles. Leave these in place as mulch to keep roots cool and moist.

• Many needles on lower branches turning brown and dropping? Too much shade on branches will cause needles to die. Prune the branches of encroaching trees or, if spacing is too tight, selectively remove trees.

• Dying ground cover under evergreens? Evergreen needles are highly acidic; few plants will grow under these trees. Try ferns or sweet woodruff or leave the ground bare.

PLANT SMART

PLANT	HEIGHT	ZONE
Fir	30'–100'	🍃 🍃 🍃
Holly	3'–50'	🍃 🍃 🍃
Pine	15'–100'	🍃 🍃 🍃 🍃
Spruce	40'–75'	🍃 🍃 🍃
Yaupon	15'–20'	🍃 🍃

FLOWERING TREES

It's like having a gigantic bouquet of flowers in your yard—and with precious little effort. Better still, many flowering trees bloom in early spring, when many yards are still looking bleak.

If you combine different trees, you'll have color in your yard for a long time. In early spring, start with the white or lilac-red REDBUD blooms, rose to white FLOWERING CHERRY blooms, then the pink-budded white CRABAPPLE. When these are fading, white and pink DOGWOODS blossom and come into full swing by mid-spring. RED HORSE CHESTNUT and cream-colored SOUTHERN MAGNOLIA carry the color into early summer. Southern magnolia has the added attractions of heady fragrance and large, glossy evergreen leaves. 'DONALD WYMAN' crabapple and FLOWERING DOGWOOD also provide winter color with long-lasting red fruits.

As with other trees, size is critical, as is a site that allows for clear viewing. The smaller flowering trees, such as 'Donald Wyman' crabapple, redbud, flowering cherry, and dogwood, can stand alone, but are even better either incorporated into a planting of flowering shrubs or anchoring one end of a flower bed. Don't be hesitant to place such plantings near patio areas or within views from windows to take advantage of their magnificent display. The southern magnolia is really big (60' to 80') and is best planted singly in lawn areas. Red horse chestnut is also large and can double as a shade tree.

Create blooming synergy in the spring with the following: 1) dogwood, 2) rhododendron, 3) lithodora, and 4) Siberian bugloss.

Flowering cherries are commonly available in weeping as well as upright forms. You can also get them with single or double pom-pom–like flowers, and in different colors: rose, pale pink, or white.

PLANT SMART

PLANT	HEIGHT	ZONE
'Donald Wyman' crabapple	10'–20'	🍃 🍃 🍃
Flowering cherry	10'–30'	🍃 🍃
Flowering dogwood	20'–30'	🍃 🍃
Red horse chestnut	30'–40'	🍃 🍃
Redbud	20'–30'	🍃 🍃 🍃
Southern magnolia	60'–80'	🍃 🍃

 CHECKLIST

SELECTION AND PLANTING

✔ To plant, see Smart Guide, page 68.

✔ Flowering crabapples are one of the most popular flowering trees, but, alas, many are disease- and insect-prone. Select varieties like 'Donald Wyman' crabapple, which is resistant to the most common problems.

✔ Some trees, such as flowering cherry, may get zapped by a very late frost. (Don't worry; while this year's display will suffer, trees should bounce back by next spring.) Where late frost is common, plant these trees in areas with a northern exposure to delay their bloom and help prevent such injury.

TROUBLE

• Trees not flowering?
1) Possibly too much shade. (Most flowering trees need sun to bloom well.) Remove some overhead branches and selectively prune branches from nearby shade-casting trees.
2) Check for poor soil with a soil test (see page 34).

• Insects nibbling on your leaves? Control most pests by spraying trees with insecticidal soap (see page 38), or call in a tree specialist certified in pesticide use.

SPECIALTY TREES

Use a small variety of red-leaved Japanese maple for dramatic color contrast in a bed of green-leaved flowering shrubs.

Want something different from the standard maple or oak? The world of trees includes an array —from weird to wonderful—of varying sizes, forms, shapes, colors, and textures. You can put that diversity to work. These "specialty" trees require little or no care once planted, except for a good drink during long dry spells.

Take the JAPANESE MAPLE. There's a Japanese maple available for almost any yard or whim. Some are large, reaching 20' and spreading just as wide, and some dwarf forms are tiny enough to fit in a large container. Leaves offer variety in color and texture, with deep red, reddish-green, or light green hues—some fine and lacy, others boldly pointed.

Consider the many dwarf varieties of normally tall evergreens. These are ideal in rock gardens or dry sunny areas of the yard because of their need for lots of sun. Even better, they require less water and other care than do many perennial flowers. Weeping or contorted pines are fun because of their unusual shapes; some can become very twisted. These should easily stand on their own in your yard.

There is color to be had with specialty trees—in their leaves, fruit, and bark. Red-leaved varieties of Japanese maple keep their color all season. 'WINTER KING' HAWTHORN has one of the best displays of red fruit in winter, and PAPERBARK MAPLE has reddish-brown bark.

If these guys are too exotic for you, consider the dwarf varieties of pine, spruce, or fir (see page 72). They make excellent easy-care foundation plantings.

SELECTING FOR
SPECIAL FEATURES

✔ For unusual form: weeping pines, dwarf evergreens

✔ For interesting bark: paperbark maple, Japanese cherry

✔ For colorful fruit: 'Winter King' hawthorn, crabapple

✔ For colorful leaves: Japanese maple, 'Sunburst' honeylocust

 • Spotting on leaves? These spots are probably caused by a fungal or bacterial disease. Spots are not usually life-threatening to the plant but merely unattractive. Ignore minor cases; for serious or ongoing problems, consult a licensed tree service.

• Leaves yellowing? Acidic soil or a lack of nutrients in the soil could be starving your tree. Have your soil tested (see page 34).

PLANT SMART

PLANT	HEIGHT	ZONE			
Japanese maple	6'–20'			🍂	🍂
Paperbark maple	20'–30'			🍂	🍂
'Sunburst' honeylocust	30'–35'	🍂	🍂	🍂	🍂
Weeping pine	2'–20'	🍂	🍂	🍂	🍂
'Winter King' hawthorn	20'–30'		🍂	🍂	🍂

(Above) Weeping pines can bend in incredible ways; use them to create a shade-producing arch over a bench.

(Left) The colorful bark of paperbark maple naturally peels away in sheetlike curls year-round.

FRUIT/NUT TREES

Apple trees (right) bear beautiful and fragrant flowers in spring and edible fruit in fall. Cherry trees (below) blossom in the spring, and blooms last for two to three weeks.

Oh, come on, even the smallest yard has room for a fruit or nut tree, especially with the availability of dwarf fruit tree varieties. It's true that these trees demand a little more attention (okay, a lot), but they pay back your efforts with fruits or nuts.

The key to success when growing fruit or nut trees is to plant them in deep, well-drained soil in the open, sunny locations of your yard. Fruit trees also require annual pruning, fertilizing, and pest control if they are to be really productive. However, the amount of care required can be drastically reduced by growing dwarf fruit trees. APPLE, PEACH, CHERRY, and citrus (LEMON, LIME, ORANGE, and GRAPEFRUIT) trees all come in smaller sizes. Because dwarfs are only 6' to 8' tall, they are easier to get at when pruning, picking, or spraying—and they still produce full-size fruit. Most fruit trees bear fruit in summer, but citrus trees produce in the winter. Note: Dwarf varieties need to be supported by staking (anchoring the trunk to a wooden stake) or training (securing trunk and branches to a sturdy fence, trellis, or wall) for the first three to four years. Semidwarfs (8' to 12') don't need staking.

WALNUT and PECAN trees are great shade trees and also provide free snacks in the summer. Plant them at least 40' from the house and other trees or obstacles, as they will reach heights of 75' and more.

SELECTION AND CARE

✔ Choose types and varieties of fruit and nut trees that are known to do well where you live. Check with your local nursery to find out.

✔ To ensure good fruit production, buy at least two varieties of a particular type of fruit tree. Remember the birds and the bees? Many fruit trees can't pollinate themselves and need a different variety nearby for cross-pollination. If you're short on space, ask for a tree with more than one variety grafted to it. Peach and many citrus trees don't need a mate.

✔ Space dwarf fruit trees 6' to 8' apart, semidwarf trees 12' apart, standard trees 16' to 18' apart, and nut trees at least 40' apart to give these trees enough room to grow.

✔ To plant, see Smart Guide, page 68.

✔ Prune fruit trees every year for best fruit production, either in late winter before buds burst or in late summer, when growth slows down. Remove enough branches to let sunlight reach developing fruit.

✔ Fertilize fruit trees every year with a standard fertilizer recommended for fruit and nut trees to sustain high yields of fruit. Nut trees can be fertilized every three to four years.

 • No fruit yet? Trees may be too young to produce fruit. On older trees, lack of fruit may be caused by excessive shade (prune nearby trees to let in light), a late frost, extended bad weather that prevents insects from pollinating trees (better luck next year), or a soil imbalance (have your soil tested; see page 34).

• Fruit dropping from trees? Some "fruit drop" is normal on such fruit trees as apple, especially if the tree produced an overabundance of fruit. Fruit drop may also occur as a result of insect infestation. Check fruit carefully for signs of bugs. You may need a more intensive pest-control program (see page 38).

• Pests? Consider alternatives to standard chemical pesticides, such as horticultural oils, insecticidal soaps, biological agents (good predatory insects), and various types of insect traps (see page 38).

PLANT SMART

PLANT	HEIGHT	ZONE
Apple	15'–25'	🍃 🍃 🍃
Cherry (sweet)	15'–40'	🍃 🍃
Citrus	15'–30'	🍃
Peach	15'–25'	🍃 🍃
Pecan	50'–100'	🍃 🍃 🍃
Walnut	50'–75'	🍃 🍃 🍃

NOTE: These heights are for standard varieties; warf and semidwarf trees range from 6' to 12'.

Walnuts ripen in shells on the tree. They will drop to the ground when ripe.

Thin out apples in late spring so the apples that remain have plenty of room to grow large and sweet.

HEDGES

When is a plant like a fence? When you plant a row of hedge plants. A hedge lets you create privacy, cut down on noise, stake out the boundary of your property, hide unsightly objects, and keep out unwanted intruders—be they four- or two-footed. Not bad for plants. In this chapter, see how smart hedges can be.

SMART GUIDE.....................................82/83

PRIVACY HEDGES..............................84/85

BOUNDARY HEDGES 86/87

CAMOUFLAGE HEDGES 88/89

HOSTILE HEDGES 90/91

HEDGE RESOURCES

American Boxwood Society 540-939-4646
Forest Farm 541-846-7269
Gurney's Seed & Nursery Co. 605-665-1671
Musser Forests Inc. 800-643-8319
Spring Hill Nurseries 800-582-8527

HEDGES

To get hedge smart, use this easy number guide to identify and name all the steps of planting and pruning a hedge. Detailed explanations of each item follow in this chapter. For information on planting hedge plants singly, see pages 94–95.

PLANTING A FORMAL HEDGE

1 . . . DIG A TRENCH AS LONG AS INTENDED HEDGE AND TWICE AS WIDE AS ROOT BALL

2 . . . PLACE PLANTS INTO TRENCH

3 . . . SPACE ACCORDING TO HEDGE PLANT TYPE

4 . . . MIX COMPOST INTO REMOVED SOIL

5 . . . BASE OF STEM (keep level with ground)

6 . . . LIGHTLY COVER PLANT ROOTS WITH SOIL MIX

7 . . . FILL TRENCH HALFWAY WITH SOIL MIX

8 . . . WATER (not shown)

9 . . . FILL TRENCH TO GROUND LEVEL WITH SOIL MIX

10 . . . WATER AGAIN

11 . . . COVER SOIL WITH MULCH (not shown)

PRUNING A SQUARED FORMAL HEDGE

12 . . . USE ELECTRIC HEDGE CLIP-PERS (see tool box)

13 . . . KEEP BASE WIDER THAN TOP

14 . . . SHEAR FLAT PLANES ON TOP AND THREE SIDES

15 . . . DO NOT PRUNE BETWEEN PLANTS

16 . . . COVER SOIL WITH MULCH ANNUALLY IN SPRING

PRUNING A ROUNDED FORMAL HEDGE

17 . . . KEEP BASE WIDER THAN TOP

18 . . . USE HAND CLIPPERS TO REMOVE ⅓ OF NEW GROWTH

19 . . . ALLOW BASES TO GROW TOGETHER

20 . . . SHAPE TOP AND SIDES TO DESIRED SHAPE

21 . . . COVER SOIL WITH MULCH ANNUALLY IN SPRING

TOOLBOX

Flat-bladed electric hedge shears work especially well on flat-sided formal hedges. Bonus: Some are cordless. Hand clippers work best for curved shapes.

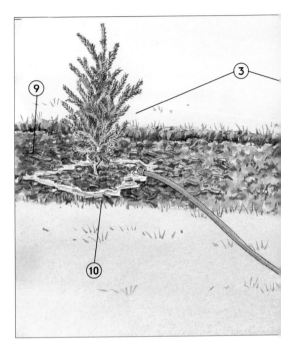

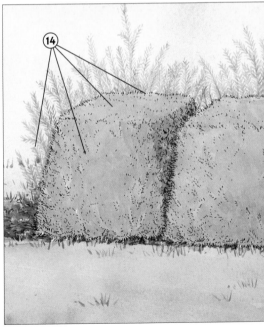

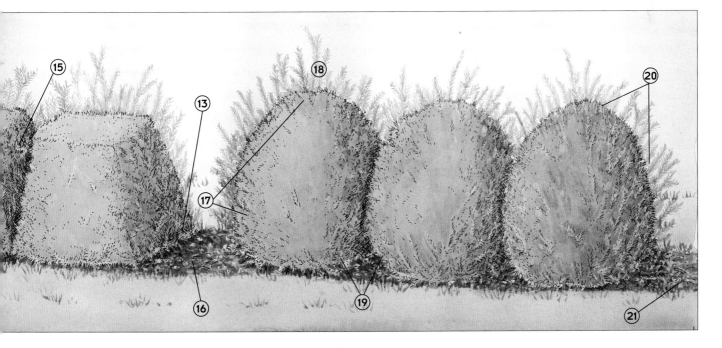

PRIVACY HEDGES

Tired of the noise or the prying eyes of uninvited observers? Then create a private garden room. By planting living walls with hedge plants, this idea can become a reality. The size of your private garden will depend on the dimensions of your yard and also on whether you want a formal or an informal hedge.

A formal hedge is one that is closely clipped to a geometric form. Formal hedges require more work than informal hedges because they have to be pruned more often. (Pruning will be easier if the hedge is made up of one type of plant.) An informal, or free-growing, hedge is allowed to develop naturally; it needs only occasional pruning to control its size and shape. Where space is an issue, plan for a formal hedge; informal hedges will take up much more room.

Hedges are easy to grow. For best effect, plant hedges in lines, either straight or curved. When selecting plants for a privacy hedge, the evergreen standards, such as CANADIAN HEMLOCK and BOXWOOD, will work well. Also consider AMERICAN CRANBERRY BUSH and CORNELIAN CHERRY; their branches are dense enough to provide privacy year-round.

Bonus: hedges come in a wide range of leaf shapes (from broad-leaved to needle-leaved), which can add a wonderful texture to a garden as well as provide a great backdrop for a flower garden.

A privacy hedge, like this one of brush cherry, should be high and dense enough to create a private space and cut down on unwanted noise.

Canadian hemlock grows well in both sun and shade. When pruning, don't repeatedly shear hedges in the same spot; this will lead to a gnarly type of growth that looks ugly.

SHORTCUTS
• If you need a hedge in a hurry, plant large specimens of evergreens. Note: The more mature the plant, the more expensive.

• Get a hedge up fast by buying fast-growing deciduous plants, such as American cranberry bush and cornelian cherry.

TROUBLE
• Lower branches thinning? Prune hedges so that the top is narrower than the bottom. This allows light to reach the lower leaves and branches and saves the hedge from developing naked limbs near the bottom.

• Harsh weather? In cold climates, wrap burlap around boxwood hedges in late fall, especially those with a southern exposure, to protect leaves from sun and wind.

CHECKLIST — SELECTION AND PLANTING

✔ For shaded areas choose PITTOSPORUM, American cranberry bush, and cornelian cherry. For sunny or shady areas, go for boxwood, YEW, HEMLOCK, or AMERICAN ARBORVITAE.

✔ Figure the length of your hedge. For a straight hedge, put a stake at both ends of the span, tie a string between the two stakes, and dig a trench. For a curved hedge, lay a piece of garden hose in the shape desired, then dig a trench along that line.

✔ For planting, see Smart Guide, page 82. Note: The planting hole for hedges should be as deep as the root ball, and twice as wide as its diameter.

✔ A rule of thumb when planting hedges: the space between each plant should be one-fourth of the hedge's full height. For example, if the hedge will grow to 8', space plants 2' apart. (If the hedge will be 4' or shorter, space plants 1' apart.)

✔ After planting, spread a 3"-deep layer of shredded wood chips, bark nuggets, or pine needles as a mulch over the soil around plants, but not against plant stems.

✔ Water a newly planted hedgerow whenever the top few inches of soil are dry. Allow the soil to dry between waterings. Don't overwater; doing so can suffocate roots.

✔ Fertilize lightly at planting, then again in 6 to 12 months. Use a slow-release or general-purpose garden fertilizer in early spring to encourage growth.

PLANT SMART

PLANT	HEIGHT	ZONE
American cranberry bush	8'–12'	🍃 🍃
Boxwood	15'–20'	🍃 🍃
Canadian hemlock	40'–70'	🍃 🍃 🍃
Cornelian cherry	20'–25'	🍃 🍃
Pittosporum	10'–12'	🍃

BOUNDARY HEDGES

Fences between neighbors don't have to be made of wood; 1) yew hedges like this create a dense wall of needlelike leaves that are easy to trim.

Using hedges as property boundaries is a good idea for a couple of reasons. 1) Hedges used to define property lines or spaces in your yard can be spaced farther apart, so you won't have to buy as many. 2) Tall shrubs or trees planted in hedgerows can be very effective windbreaks, which in colder regions can have a significant effect on reducing winter heating bills. Also, windbreaks can reduce the drying effect of wind on soil. (That means you won't have to water as often.)

More good news: hedges used as boundaries don't have to be pruned to formal shapes. Taller plants, such as AMERICAN HOLLY, can be left to develop their natural form. For shaded areas, and if height is not a consideration, CHERRY LAUREL is a good choice. If BLACK HAW or another flowering shrub is used to define borders, leave it unpruned to allow the best development and display of flowers. Only in small yards, where space is limited, will a hedge really need to be pruned to keep it at a narrow width. In this case, select a plant that takes close clipping—for example, CALIFORNIA PRIVET.

SELECTION AND PLANTING

✔ Decide whether you want deciduous or evergreen plants: black haw and California privet are deciduous plants. Cherry laurel, American holly, American arborvitae, and yew are evergreens.

✔ If you need an instant boundary, choose fast-growing plants, such as California privet. Note: Fast-growing hedges often have a shorter life span than slower-growing types and may require more care.

✔ Flowering shrubs make great boundary hedges. Try hydrangeas (see page 96) or shrub roses (see page 102).

✔ When buying plants for a hedge, look for those with dense branching and no obvious gaps in the interior of the plant.

✔ For instructions on planting a hedge, see Smart Guide, page 82.

✔ Don't place a hedge right on top of your property line. If you do, a good portion of the hedge will be on your neighbor's property—and subject to his or her will.

PLANT SMART

PLANT	HEIGHT	ZONE		
American arborvitae	40'–60'	●	●	●
American holly	40'–60'		●	●
Black haw	12'–15'	●	●	●
California privet	10'–15'		●	●
Cherry laurel	10'–18'			●
Yew	2'–60'	●	●	●

 ## TROUBLE

• Brown sections of evergreen hedges appearing in late winter or early spring? Evergreen hedges—such as American arborvitae, American holly, and cherry laurel—are prone to the drying effects of wintry winds and bright sunlight in early spring. Water in early fall, then again when soil thaws. (Consider spraying evergreens with an antidesiccant, which coats the needles and leaves with a thin film of plastic to seal in moisture. Do this in early winter or during warm spells during mid- and late winter.)

• Weeds beneath your hedgerow? Placing a 2" to 3" layer of mulch (wood chips, pine bark, pine needles) beneath hedges will keep most weeds in check.

Plant low-growing (2' to 4') hedges, like this 1) spreading yew to set a boundary and still preserve the view—in this case the river.

CAMOUFLAGE HEDGES

Evergreen Italian cypresses, which are very tall and narrow, can hide something as large as the neighbor's house while also allowing some light to filter into your property.

We all have something to hide. It may be a propane-gas tank, electrical meters, or trash cans. Hedges are ideal for camouflaging or concealing unsightly structures because the plants blend so well with the surrounding landscape. A solid wooden fence, on the other hand, stands out starkly from the natural landscape.

For objects that need to be hidden from view year-round, evergreens are your best bet because they don't lose their leaves. Good news: you don't have to plant many—just enough to block the most likely lines of sight between you and the offending object.

The height of the hedge is especially important if the hedge is to be effective. For most people, a 6'-tall hedge will be above eye level, but check vantage points in your yard to see whether you need a taller hedge. If you need a hedge that is only about 6' to 10' tall, use JAPANESE HOLLY or FRASER PHOTINIA. For hedges taller than 10', try EASTERN RED CEDAR or LEYLAND CYPRESS.

Shearing off most of the new growth at the top and along the sides will confine the plants for a long time, but no plant should be kept at the same width forever; plants need to be able to expand to stay healthy. Prune lightly.

PLANT SMART

PLANT	HEIGHT	ZONE
Chinese juniper (columnar forms)	50'–60'	
Eastern red cedar (columnar forms)	40'–50'	
Fraser photinia	10'–15'	
Italian cypress	20'–30'	
Japanese holly	5'–10'	
Leyland cypress	60'–70'	

Boxwood is a great shrub for hiding objects, especially since it remains green all year long. However, don't use it to hide important safety items like fire hydrants or traffic signs.

CHECKLIST

SELECTION AND CARE

✔ Stand at various points in your yard to estimate the approximate height and length of hedge you need.

✔ To calculate how many plants you'll need, use the following as a rule of thumb: The space between each plant should be one-fourth of the hedge's full height. Plants in an 8' juniper hedge, then, should be spaced 2' apart, from stem to stem. If your hedgerow will be 20' long, buy 10 plants.

✔ To plant, see Smart Guide, page 82.

✔ Prune formal camouflage hedges once a year to keep them thick. For informal hedges, cut back some top and side branches each year to help keep shrubs thick and dense.

✔ Spread a 2" to 3" layer of wood bark chips beneath the plants. The mulch keeps the soil moist and weed-free.

SHORTCUTS

• If you have enough space, create informal hedges of Leyland cypress, Fraser photinia, or juniper as a screen; they require less annual care, particularly pruning.

• Hedge plants used for privacy hedges, such as boxwood and Canadian hemlock, also camouflage objects well.

TROUBLE

• Pale needles on evergreen shrubs? Sucking insects, such as spider mites, can leave plant foliage looking rather anemic. Examine plants regularly for spider mites and other insect pests. Apply horticultural oils or insecticidal soap to eliminate them (see page 38).

• Sparse-looking sections in your hedge? This could mean that your hedge is not tolerant of shade. Try pruning the branches of any trees casting shade. Best plants for shady areas: Fraser photinia, yews, and hemlocks.

HOSTILE HEDGES

Rugosa rose hedges are far more attractive than fences but perform the same function because of their thorns. Rugosas are easy to grow, disease-resistant, and do not need to be pruned often.

Here's a thorny subject. Want to deter unwanted visitors from your property (whether of the two- or the four-legged variety)? Or simply stop pedestrians from taking shortcuts at the corner of your yard? Create an impenetrable hedge.

First, select shrubs that normally produce many stems at their base, such as RUGOSA ROSE and JAPANESE BARBERRY. With close planting (keep a space of about 20" to 24" between each plant) and regular pruning, these shrubs can produce a very dense growth that will keep most larger animals (not to mention humans) from pushing through. Another solution: plant a double row of shrubs.

Now for the thorns: plant a hedge of WASHINGTON HAWTHORN, rugosa rose, FIRE THORN, or KANGAROO THORN. Thanks to their thorns, these plants can be very effective where security is a concern; merely the sight of such a hedge is enough to cause one to make alternative plans.

To keep shortcutters from trampling your lawn, you don't need a high, imposing hedge. Sometimes the strategic location of one short, thorny plant, such as Japanese barberry, at a corner of your property can redirect transgressors to walkways while also acting as a focal point in your yard.

CHECKLIST SELECTION AND PLANTING

✔ If you want a green hedge all year long, choose the evergreens fire thorn and kangaroo thorn. If you choose deciduous hedge plants, such as Washington hawthorn, rugosa rose, and Japanese barberry, you'll see branches and thorns in winter.

✔ Don't plant thorny hedges if you have kids or pets who could be harmed by the thorns when playing outside.

✔ It will be easier to plant thorny things if you start with small seedlings (about 12" tall). (Larger specimens of such thorny hedges as Washington hawthorn and fire thorn can be nasty to handle because of their thorns.) Regardless of the size of plants, wear leather gloves and long-sleeved shirts when planting.

✔ To plant, see Smart Guide, page 82.

✔ For established thick, impenetrable hedges, cut the stems back by a third to promote branching at the base of the plant. As the plants grow, continue to cut back new shoots by one-third in late fall or early spring.

 TROUBLE • Hedges have become too large? To restore an overgrown hedge, cut stems back in early spring to about 12" above the ground and allow to regrow.

• Animals still getting through the lower parts of barrier hedges? Tuck chicken wire or other wire fencing between plants in the hedgerow.

 SHORTCUTS • For large hedges, save money and buy small bare-root plants (see Smart Guide, page 82). These plants are usually no more than 12" to 18" tall and won't take long to become established. Order them from mail-order nurseries; ask about quantity discounts.

PLANT SMART

PLANT	HEIGHT	ZONE
Fire thorn	6'–18'	🍃🍃
Japanese barberry	3'–6'	🍃🍃
Kangaroo thorn	to 10'	🍃
Rugosa rose	4'–6'	🍃🍃🍃
Washington hawthorn	25'–30'	🍃🍃🍃

A curbside fire thorn guarantees no trespassers in the yard. This evergreen also adds bright color in fall and winter.

FLOWERING SHRUBS

Hardy as trees, pretty as flowers. Better still decorative shrubs can hide the foundation and set off key parts of your yard with color. What more could you want? And they are so simple to plant and care for. Find out just how easy it can be to add a little color to your yard.

SMART GUIDE....................................94/95

HYDRANGEAS...................................96/97

RHODODENDRONS/AZALEAS 98/99

VIBURNUMS....................................100/101

SHRUB ROSES 102/103

FLOWERING VINES........................104/105

FLOWERING SHRUBS

To get plant smart, use this easy number guide to identify and name all the steps to planting and growing flowering vines and shrubs. For information on planting as hedges, see pages 82–83.

PLANTING VINES

1 . . . DIG HOLE TWICE AS WIDE AS PLANT ROOT

2 . . . PLACE PLANT IN HOLE

3 . . . MIX COMPOST INTO REMOVED SOIL AND COVER PLANT ROOTS

4 . . . BASE OF STEM (keep level with ground)

5 . . . FILL WITH SOIL TO GROUND LEVEL (not shown)

6 . . . COVER SOIL WITH MULCH (not shown)

GROWING VINES

7 . . . VINE PLANTED AT BASE OF LAMP POST

8 . . . TACK STRING TO POST TO CREATE SUPPORT

9 . . . ENTWINE VINE AROUND STRING

10 . . . MULCH, TO KEEP ROOTS COOL AND MOIST IN SUN

11 . . . PRUNE OR TRAIN NEW GROWTH

PLANTING SHRUBS

12 . . . DIG HOLE TWICE AS WIDE AS ROOT BALL

13 . . . FIELD-GROWN PLANT (balled and burlapped)

14 . . . BURLAP (can be left around roots; untie and spread open in hole)

15 . . . CONTAINER PLANT

16 . . . CUT CONTAINER AWAY

17 . . . PLANT SHRUB

18 . . . BASE OF STEM (keep level with ground)

19 . . . FILL TO GROUND LEVEL WITH SOIL AND COMPOST

20 . . . WATER (not shown)

21 . . . COVER SOIL WITH MULCH (not shown)

PRUNING OVERGROWN SHRUB

22 . . . DESIRED SHAPE

23 . . . OVERGROWN STEMS

24 . . . SELECT ONE-THIRD OF SHRUB STEMS AND PRUNE BACK TO DESIRED SHAPE

25 . . . REPEAT PRUNING FOR TWO MORE YEARS

26 . . . COVER WITH MULCH ANNUALLY IN SPRING

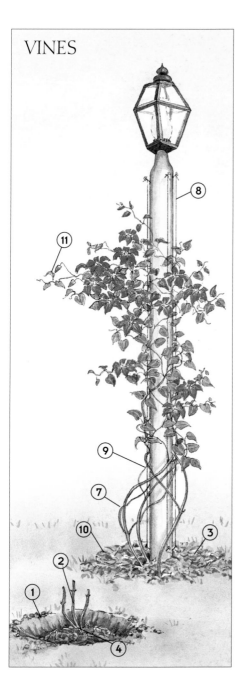

VINES

PLANTING SHRUBS

PRUNING SHRUBS

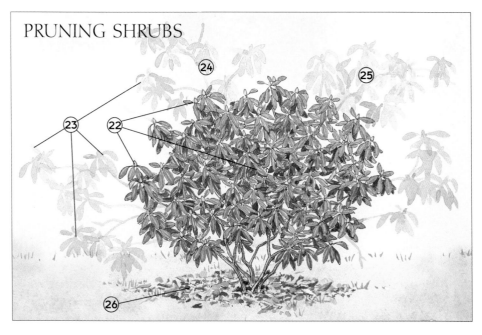

CONTAINER VS. BALLED AND BURLAPPED?

Price and size are the two main considerations. As their name implies, container-grown plants spend their youth in a container. They are sold young and therefore come small and are less expensive.

Balled and burlapped ("b and b") shrubs are grown in the ground (field grown). They are larger, older, and therefore more expensive than container plants. They come with roots wrapped in burlap.

HYDRANGEAS

Fast-growing bigleaf hydrangeas are one of the top choices for prettying up a yard in a hurry. They are great for informal hedges, as well as for planting in front of foundations.

Hydrangeas in bloom are show-stoppers. For that reason, you'll often find them gracing the front of a house or a walkway.

There are three popular types of hydrangeas. The first is the BIGLEAF. It has two flower forms: huge round clusters and lacy flat clusters. Both bloom in summer and typically grow almost as high as wide—usually 3' to 6', but sometimes 10'. Flower color can change with the pH of the soil (see page 34). For blue flowers, keep the soil acidic (pH of between 5.0 and 5.5); a soil pH of 6.0 to 7.0 gives pink blossoms.

PANICLE hydrangeas are leaner, have a V shape, and grow taller than bigleafs. In summer, they feature huge clusters of antique-white blossoms that turn russet-red in fall. When the flowers bloom, they are white, no matter what the acidity of the soil.

The last type is the CLIMBING hydrangea. Yes, it really does climb, and it is widely acclaimed as the best clinging vine available, bar none. It can grow up to 80' high and branch out 3' on each side of the main stem. That's big. Be patient, as it takes a couple of years to get started.

All hydrangeas like rich, moist soil that drains well. Most will thrive in partial shade or full sun. All hydrangeas are deciduous: they lose their leaves in the winter.

PLANTING AND CARE

✔ All hydrangeas can be purchased in containers. Climbers usually come staked.

✔ Give hydrangeas lots of elbowroom. Space bigleafs 3' to 6' apart, panicles 8' to 15' apart. Climbers should be planted 4' to 5' away from a wall or fence.

✔ Dig a hole twice as wide and the same depth as the size of the root ball. Toss organic matter (compost or peat moss) into the hole and also mix it into the soil taken from the hole. Position the plant so that the base of the stem is at ground level, and gently pack soil around the roots. Once it's planted, water the hydrangea thoroughly and fertilize.

✔ Prune bigleaf hydrangeas immediately after flowering to maintain the shrub's desired shape. Prune panicles in late winter or early spring before growth begins. Climbers don't need pruning, except to shape them.

Bigleafs are hearty and will grow along or above rocky foundations. In fact, against south-facing walls, the sun on the stone will warm hydrangeas and help them thrive in marginal zones.

• Bloom color not what you expected? New concrete foundation materials can leach into the soil and make it less acidic. Test soil acidity and amend as needed (see page 34).

• Powdery white mildew on the leaves? Spray your shrubs with the appropriate fungicide (see page 38) at the first sign of mildew.

HYDRANGEA NURSERY SOURCES

Carroll Gardens 800-638-6334

Spring Hill
Nurseries 800-582-8527

Wayside Gardens . . 800-845-1124

White Flower Farm . 800-503-9624

PLANT SMART

PLANT	HEIGHT	ZONE
Bigleaf	3'–6'	
Climbing	2'–80'	
Panicle	8'–15'	

Climbing hydrangeas are so strong and heavy they can pull down a flimsy support. Give them sturdy fences, walls, or trees to climb on. Their reddish-brown bark is attractive in winter.

RHODODENDRONS/AZALEAS

Azaleas come in a range of wonderful bright colors. Plant them in informal, hedgelike rows to provide privacy from the street or the neighbors.

Think superlow maintenance and exuberant color with these two favorites. Bonus: most rhododendrons (or "rhodies," as they are called in the nursery biz) are evergreen, with glossy dark leaves that stay attractive year-round. Azaleas, on the other hand, shed some of their leaves in fall, but thanks to creative botany, there are a number of evergreen hybrids, such as the ROBIN HILL HYBRIDS.

Rhododendrons and azaleas share many of the same growing requirements. Maybe that's because they are close relatives; in botany-land, azaleas *are* rhododendrons. Both flourish in moist, acidic soil. Although they grow well in full sun, the blooms last longer and keep a richer color in partial shade (preferably, afternoon shade). Actually, all

they need is four hours of direct sunlight a day to help them produce enough buds for a stupendous display.

There are thousands of varieties of these shrubs, and they come in many sizes to suit any garden site. At the small end are the large-flowered Robin Hill azalea hybrids, only 1' to 2' tall. At the tall end, ROSEBAY rhodies are usually 10' to 15' high, but can reach 30' in ideal sites; their flowers are generally white to rose or lilac-rose. The many varieties of CATAWBA rhodies range from yellow and salmon to lavender-blue; FORTUNEI HYBRID rhodies are red to pale pink. GLENN DALE HYBRID azaleas have some of the largest flowers and come in a spectrum of colors, often with darker spots or stripes. KURUME HYBRID and Robin Hill azaleas display hues of lilac, salmon, pink, and red.

BUYING, PLANTING, AND CARE

✔ Rhododendrons and azaleas come either in containers or balled and burlapped ("b & b," in the trade). Be sure to peel away the burlap before planting (remove it completely if it's made of a synthetic material). For planting instructions, see page 94.

✔ When buying these shrubs, read the tag. Some will carry a three-number designation from the American Rhododendron Society that indicates flower quality (first number), foliage quality (second number), and the overall quality of the shrub (third number). On a scale of 1 to 5, 5 is best.

✔ Rhododendrons and azaleas need a more acidic soil than many other plants to grow well. Test your soil (see page 34) and add sulfur as needed to keep the pH level between 4.5 and 5.5. Add a shovelful of pine needles or coffee grounds to the soil to help acidify it.

Don't be afraid to relocate an azalea if it outgrows its site. With their shallow and fibrous roots, azaleas are relatively easy to move.

✔ Place them at a healthy distance from plants with lots of surface roots (birches and maples) so that their roots don't have to compete for water and nutrients in the soil.

✔ Use a fertilizer designed for acid-loving plants.

✔ Don't overdo the pruning. Annual pruning is unnecessary for rhododendrons and azaleas. If you must prune, do so only right after plants finish flowering. Cut minimally—just a light overall trim to restore the plant to optimal shape or size.

PLANT SMART

PLANT	HEIGHT	ZONE	
RHODODENDRONS			
Catawba	6'–12'	🍃	🍃
Fortunei hybrids	3'–8'		🍃
Rosebay	10'–15'	🍃	🍃
AZALEAS			
Glenn Dale hybrids	4'–6'	🍃	🍃
Kurume hybrids	4'–6'		🍃
Robin Hill hybrids	1'–2'	🍃	🍃

Make the most of next year's blooms by pinching off old and faded flowers. The shrub will focus on forming buds, not seeds.

RHODODENDRON/ AZALEA RESOURCES

American Rhododendron Society 707-725-3043

Brown's Kalmia & Azalea 360-371-5551

Greer Gardens 800-548-0111

Musser Forests 800-643-8319

Shepard Hill Farm 914-528-5917

VIBURNUMS

The doublefile viburnum's flowers bloom in clusters. The plant's horizontal branches help to make it a great centerpiece for any garden.

Ah, viburnums—those nice big bushes that range in height from 2' to 30' with huge white flowers. They can offer three seasons' worth of benefits: flowers in spring, plentiful green foliage in summer, and colorful berries and leaves in fall. Bonus: the berries also will attract songbirds. Viburnums even tolerate clay or poorly drained soil. They are easy to grow, and, once they're established, you can sit back and enjoy them with barely a thought toward care. Look for 8" to 12" of growth a year.

Viburnums work well clustered, all alone, or in a border of different shrubs. For maximum enjoyment, plant sweet-scented KOREAN SPICE viburnum where its perfume will waft your way often—under a window or framing a deck. Its scent is strongest on humid evenings.

Viburnums come in many varieties. Most shed their leaves, but LAURUSTINUS and DAVID are evergreen. Most viburnums need moist, well-drained, and slightly acidic soil. All viburnums can be grown in either sun or partial shade, but sun encourages better flowers and fruit.

PLANT SMART

PLANT	HEIGHT	ZONE
American cranberry bush	8'–10'	🍃 🍃 🍃
David	3'–5'	🍃
Doublefile	8'–10'	🍃 🍃
Korean spice	4'–8'	🍃 🍃
Laurustinus	6'–12'	🍃 🍃

TROUBLE

• No pretty fall fruits on bushes? Plant two or more viburnums of the same type together to ensure that flowers get pollinated and form colorful fruits.

• Disfigured leaves on your shrubs? Aphids, thrips, mites, and scale can cause yellowed or shriveled leaves unless they are treated with the proper insecticide. (Ask your local garden center for the right type.)

All viburnums offer attractive blossoms, but David (above) has glossy green, pleated-looking leaves that last all year long. They are just the right size to edge a patio.

SELECTION, PLANTING, CARE

CHECKLIST

✔ Choose a shrub that stands up straight in its container and isn't loose or wobbly. Look for branches that are well balanced.

The berries of many Viburnum varieties are red, but some form blue, black, orange, or yellow berries. This variety has red berries at first, which later darken to blue. Don't eat these; they are not edible.

✔ If you're a mail-order shopper, pass up Korean spice viburnums. This type grows much better if bought from your local nursery in a container or with burlap-wrapped soil around its roots. Mail-order shrubs generally come with no soil around their roots ("bare-root").

✔ For planting instructions, see page 94.

✔ Viburnums rarely need pruning. Their naturally graceful, spreading shape looks best with only the lightest pruning. (If a plant is totally overgrown, cut it down to a few inches above the ground. This tough-love treatment will forfeit the next year's bloom, but the following year's display should be worth the price. The plant will grow back to its original height in about three years.)

VIBURNUM NURSERY SOURCES

Carroll
Gardens Inc. 800-638-6334

Wayside
Gardens 800-845-1124

White Flower
Farm 800-503-9624

SHRUB ROSES

Shrub roses work well as hedges, trained up a trellis or the side of a house, and in the middle of a flower or shrub border. This garden features 'White Meidiland', valued because it blooms all summer long.

Turned off by the intense pruning, spraying, and feeding that you've heard roses require? Then take these two words when you go shopping: *shrub roses*. Shrub roses are the hardiest, easiest roses to grow—honest. Although shrub roses prefer rich, slightly acidic soil, they can get by with much less. In fact, many seem to thrive on neglect, tolerating salty air, road de-icing salts, and soil that would send their more delicate relations into a swoon. Just give them an open, sunny spot and you're done.

Shrub roses are divided into groups containing varieties in a slew of sizes and colors—from whites to yellows, pinks, and reds. In May and June, FATHER HUGO'S ROSE (an old favorite) is covered with five-petaled butter-yellow blooms. Many other roses bloom again after early-summer display. Hardy MEIDILANDS™ bloom longest. ENGLISH ROSES have large blossoms that will remind you of your grandma's. HYBRID MUSKS are very fragrant, as are many others. Bonus: after blooming, rugged RUGOSAS display hard red fruit (called hips) well into winter.

BUYING, PLANTING, AND CARE

✔ You can buy shrub roses from mail-order nurseries and rose specialists either with bare roots (before leaves appear) or in containers.

✔ Plant roses as you would other shrubs; see page 94.

PLANT SMART

PLANT	HEIGHT	ZONE
English rose hybrids	3'–6'	
Father Hugo's	6'–10'	
Hybrid musk	6'–8'	
Meidiland	2'–5'	
Rugosa (and hybrids)	4'–6'	

✔ When buds start to swell in spring, give rose plants just a light pruning: remove any dead canes (rose stems) and, on older bushes, one or two of the thicker, older canes.

✔ After roses bloom, cut back long canes by one-third. Snip off faded flowers early in the season to encourage more blooms (this is called "deadheading").

✔ To keep blooms coming, feed shrub roses with a balanced liquid fertilizer, such as fish emulsion, every two to three weeks, from spring until midsummer. Don't feed late in the season or you'll make plants more susceptible to winter dieback (dead branches caused by cold temperatures).

✔ To dry roses, cut when they are open three-quarters of the way, in the cool of the morning. Bring inside and hang upside down with string in a cool, dimly lit room for a week to 10 days.

The hips of the rugosa rose can be cooked and made into rose hip jelly.

• Spots appearing on leaves? Possible problems: 1) Plants may be too crowded to allow good air circulation. Dig up crowded plants and replant, spacing them a little farther apart. 2) Too much watering at night. Water roses early in the morning so leaves can dry off before nightfall.

• Icky-looking buds? Midges, thrips, or other insect pests are at work. Cut off severely damaged buds to prevent pests from spreading.

ROSE RESOURCES

American Rose
Society 800-637-6534

Jackson & Perkins . . .800-872-7673

The Roseraie at
Bayfields 207-832-6330

Spring Hill
Nurseries 800-582-8527

White
Flower Farm 800-503-9624

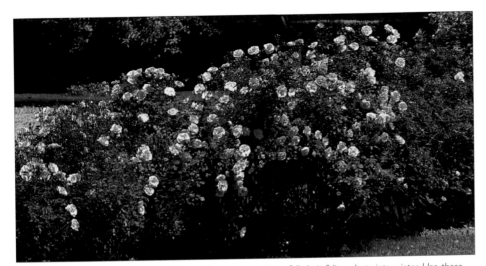

'Bonica' roses, of the Meidiland group, bloom all summer and into fall; their foliage lasts into winter. Use these roses to create hedges, to hide house foundations, or in masses on their own.

FLOWERING VINES

Perennial flowering vines (or climbers) are clever additions to a yard because, with them, you can grow towering masses of flowers in a spot as small as one square foot. Whether you twine vines up a mailbox, arbor, chain-link fence, or screen that disguises an eyesore, they can dazzle you with color—from hot pink or purple (BOUGAINVILLEA) to orange-red (TRUMPET CREEPER) to cool white (JASMINE). CLEMATIS comes in a Popsicle range of colors. Best of all, vines grow fast.

Choose a vine that suits your climate: bougainvillea and jasmine do well in warm climates; WISTERIA, trumpet creeper, and clematis are popular in the country's midsection; and different types of HONEYSUCKLE thrive in different climes, from the warmest to the coldest.

Although vines are a diverse group, most are easy to grow and take care of, once established. All bloom best in full sun, although clematis is much happier if its roots are shaded (by other plants or, at least, by lots of mulch).

Clematis, jasmine, and honeysuckle need narrow supports around which they can climb. Huge wisterias need strong, sturdy supports to twine around. Trumpet creepers cling to just about anything; you may want to install a sturdy trellis to keep them from pulling the siding down. Bougainvillea is careless as it climbs and scrambles all over; tie it to its support.

If you've got a new house surrounded by tiny young shrubs, use a vine or two (like this snow-white 'Henryi' clematis) to give your property instant character.

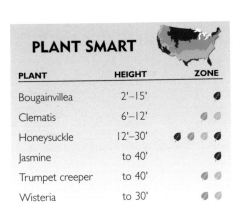

The thick, viny stems of purple wisteria need strong support, in this case a wooden bridge and the stem of a doublefile viburnum.

 SELECTION, PLANTING, CARE

✔ Vines may take hold more quickly if you buy them in containers from your local nursery. On dormant (leafless) vines, look for plump, firm buds; on growing plants, look for healthy leaves. If you can't find what you want, buy mail-order—but you'll probably get smaller plants.

✔ Plant vines the way you would a shrub or tree (see pages 94 and 68). Clematis, jasmine, and bougainvillea prefer fertile soil that has a lot of organic matter; wisteria, trumpet creeper, and honeysuckle can take any soil that is not soggy.

✔ Feed clematis, jasmine, and bougainvillea once a year, as growth starts in spring. (The others don't need fertilizer unless the soil is extremely poor; too much nitrogen will reduce the number of blooms.)

✔ To control the size of vines, prune annually. Prune spring-blooming vines just after flowering. For those that bloom in summer, prune in late winter or early spring before new growth emerges.

Prune large-blossomed types, which flower on new growth, in late winter or early spring. Prune small-flowered types right after they bloom, to keep them from sprawling.

• Infertile soil? Pick trumpet creeper or one of the honeysuckles. They'll grow in almost any soil and in partial shade. They'll also tolerate drought and neglect.

 • If you want to attract hummingbirds, plant trumpet creeper or honeysuckle. These birds love the fragrant, bright-colored flowers.

PLANT SMART

PLANT	HEIGHT	ZONE
Bougainvillea	2'–15'	🍃
Clematis	6'–12'	🍃 🍃
Honeysuckle	12'–30'	🍃 🍃 🍃 🍃
Jasmine	to 40'	🍃
Trumpet creeper	to 40'	🍃 🍃
Wisteria	to 30'	🍃 🍃

TROUBLE • Foliage looking thin? If leaves look sparse at the roots but bushy at the top, force new growth to develop lower down by pinching back the tops of the stems.

• Trumpet creeper taking over your yard? Remove the seedlings as soon as they appear (they look like baby versions of the big vines). Plant this vine well away from shrub and flower gardens.

• Shrinking clematis flowers? Your vine may need to be refreshed with a light pruning (cut stems back to just above a fat bud).

FLOWERING VINE NURSERY SOURCES

Milaegar's
Gardens Inc.. 414-639-2040

Miller
Nurseries Inc.. 800-836-9630

Spring Hill
Nurseries 800-582-8527

Thompson &
Morgan 800-274-7333

White Flower Farm . 800-503-9624

EASY FLOWERS

Start out easy with annuals. You plant them in spring, they continue to bloom during summer, and then, when the cold comes, they're gone for good. Next, try bulbs, which bloom for years. Then, when you've mastered bulbs, go on to perennials—these flowers make your garden permanent because they bloom year in and year out. When you're *really* ready, you can mix all three.

SMART GUIDE.................................108/109

ANNUALS 110/113

BULBS 114/117

PERENNIALS 118/123

EASY FLOWERS

To get flower smart, use this easy number guide to identify and name all the processes of planting. Detailed explanations of each item follow in this chapter.

ANNUALS

1 . . . DIG HOLE TWICE AS WIDE AS PLANT ROOTS

2 . . . REMOVE FLOWER FROM PLASTIC FLAT

3 . . . PLANT FLOWER IN HOLE, FILL WITH SOIL

4 . . . WATER WELL (not shown)

5 . . . COVER SOIL WITH MULCH (not shown)

6 . . . STAGGER PLACEMENT OF FLOWERS

BULBS

7 . . . BULB PLANTER TOOL

8 . . . DIG HOLE THREE TIMES AS DEEP AS HEIGHT OF BULB

9 . . . PLACE BULBS IN HOLE, POINTED-END UP (root-end down)

10 . . . SPACE 4"-8" APART

11 . . . COVER WITH SOIL (not shown)

12 . . . WATER (not shown)

13 . . . CORM

14 . . . BULB

15 . . . SCALY BULB

PERENNIALS

16 . . . DIG HOLE TWICE AS WIDE AS ROOTS (not shown)

17 . . . PLANT FLOWER LEVEL WITH GROUND, COVER WITH SOIL; WATER (not shown)

18 . . . COVER SOIL WITH MULCH

19 . . . PLANT LARGE PERENNIALS 2'–3' APART

20 . . . FIBROUS ROOTS

21 . . . TUBEROUS ROOTS

22 . . . FLESHY CYLINDRICAL ROOTS

23 . . . DIVIDE TUBEROUS ROOTS BY SLICING A LARGE CLUMP (using a spade)

COLOR SMART

In sunny gardens, go with bright, vivid colors: reds, oranges, pinks. In cooler, shadier gardens, stick to cool colors: blues, purples, silvers. Don't forget to use white flowers; they go with everything.

ANNUALS

BULBS

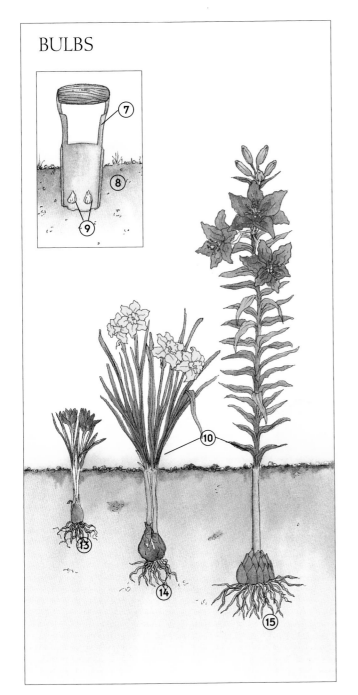

PERENNIALS

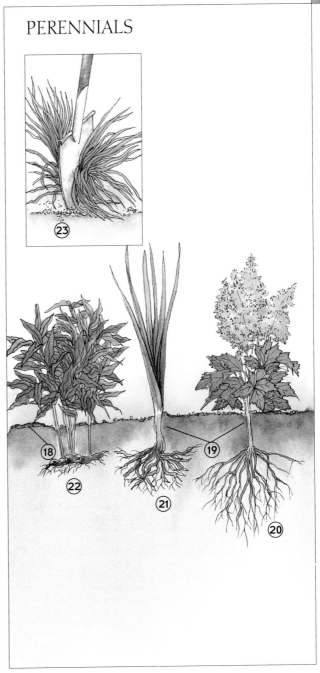

SMART GUIDE

ANNUALS

This flower bed is planted with a mix of annuals, bulbs, and perennials for three seasons of color. In spring the following bulbs will bloom: 1) tulip, 2) crocus, 3) hyacinth, and 4) daffodil. In addition, annuals like 5) marigold and 6) pansy will flower as soon as planted. And perennials like 7) forget-me-not, 8) iris, and 9) peony will be starting to flower. The same bed can be planted so that it will continue blooming in summer (see page 114) and fall (see page 118).

Annuals are flowering plants that last for a year (hence the name "annual"). They bloom in late spring through summer and then fade and die when cool weather comes—you can dig them up and discard them then. You can buy annuals in four- or six-container plastic packs from your local nursery or garden center.

What to look for when buying annuals: don't buy a plant that *is* in bloom. Take note of others of the same type that are, but buy those that are just budding. At this size, the roots aren't spilling out of their containers and the plants aren't too "leggy"—overly tall for their height range. Leggy plants or those with yellow leaves have peaked in growth before they should have and will quickly sputter out in your yard.

Now, before you go out and start buying, you need to know about something called *hardiness*—a plant's ability to handle cold. *Hardy* annuals can cope with some frost before expiring; *half-hardy* annuals can handle cold weather, but not frost; and *tender* annuals do not like cold weather and will die in frost.

When to plant? Here's an easy rule of thumb: in the North plant your annuals in late spring, when frost season is over; in the South plant in late winter or early spring. Note: Annuals are ideal plants for containers (aka fancy pots); see page 134.

Impatiens provide tidy mounds of nonstop color, quickly fill in a flower bed, and are one of the few annuals that prefer shade. Unlike most annuals, you don't have to cut off their dead blooms to keep flowers coming.

OTHER ANNUALS

HARDY TYPES:
Black-eyed Susan
Cornflower
Larkspur
Snapdragon

HALF-HARDY TYPES:
African daisy
Cosmos
Nasturtium
Petunia
Poppy

TENDER TYPES:
Celosia
China aster
Flowering tobacco
Heliotrope
Portulaca

BEGONIA

The begonia most often grown as an annual is called the WAX BEGONIA because of its shiny leaves. These perky plants grow from 6" to 8" high and come in eye-catching shades of red, pink, and white. They're great as an edging or in window boxes or hanging baskets.

• Wax begonias like sunny or shady spots; the best spot gets a mixture of both. Grow in fertile, well-drained soil.

• To plant, dig a hole large enough to hold plant roots. Space 6" to 8" apart. Water right after planting, then twice a week throughout your growing season.

IMPATIENS

These tender annuals range from 6" to 18" in height, which makes them ideal in beds around tree trunks and along walkways. They come in white, red, yellow, and pink. You can mass single colors or mix and match for a multicolored effect.

• Impatiens grow best in partial shade in fertile, well-drained soil.

• To plant, dig a hole large enough to hold plant roots. Space 6" to 12" apart, or check nursery tag for instructions. Impatiens fill in and spread out quickly, so be prepared for instant success. Water thoroughly after planting, then twice a week throughout your growing season.

Begonias 1) offer showy, vibrant flowers with dark foliage. Plant them in containers or mix red and pink ones in your garden with white flowers for contrast.

ANNUALS CONT'D

Cheerful orange-and-yellow marigolds can help keep bugs away from your vegetable garden.

 • Wilted annuals? You probably didn't water deeply enough. Check the moisture of the soil by inserting a wooden Popsicle stick in the soil 2" to 3". If it comes out dry, water the soil thoroughly.

• Started annuals from seeds and they didn't sprout? It's easier to start plants from seedlings (baby plants). Buy these from a nursery and pop them in the ground in spring.

• Bugs eating your annuals? If it's just one plant, remove it. If bugs are everywhere, take a damaged stem to your local nursery. They'll identify the culprit and tell you what to do.

MARIGOLD

Half-hardy marigolds range in height from 6" to 36". The flowers bloom in snowball shapes and come in harvest colors of yellow, red, and orange as well as white. Bonus: the stems grow thick with leaves that are heavily scented—a sort of earthy aroma.

• Marigolds thrive in a range of soils, from moist to dry, and flower best in full sun. Some afternoon shade keeps the flowers fresher for longer.

• To plant, dig a hole large enough to hold plant roots. Space small types 6" apart and large ones 15" apart. Plant in warm soil, after the danger of frost has passed. Water thoroughly after planting, then twice a week throughout your growing season.

PANSY

This superhardy garden favorite ranges in height from 6" to 9". The five-petaled flowers come in a wide range of colors, from cool blues and purples to hot reds, oranges, and yellows. Bonus: the flower petals can be a single color or two toned with a dark, slightly irregular center—what gardeners call "facelike."

• Pansies grow best in full sun in cool regions and partial shade in warm places. They like moist, fertile, well-drained soil.

• To plant, dig a hole large enough to hold plant roots. Space 6" to 8" apart. Water thoroughly after planting, then twice a week throughout your growing season.

Pansies are short little flowers, making them ideal for edging borders or the rims of containers.

SALVIA

These half-hardy annuals are actually ornamental sages that are topped with spear-shaped clusters of red, purple, pink, or white flowers. Salvias range in height from 1' to 2'. They're good for prettying up a fence or in the center of a flower bed.

• Salvias like full sun to partial shade. Grow in well-drained, moist soil.

• To plant, dig a hole large enough to hold plant roots. Space 6" to 12" apart. Water thoroughly after planting, then twice a week throughout your growing season.

Red salvia's 1) upright spikes contrast with the rounded form of open, petaled flowers.

Zinnias offer big, bold color and make nice cutting flowers for indoor arrangements.

PLANT SMART		
PLANT	**HEIGHT**	**ZONE**
Begonia (wax)	6"–8"	
Impatiens	6"–18"	
Marigold	6"–36"	
Pansy	6"–9"	
Salvia	12"–24"	
Zinnia	8"–30"	

ZINNIA

Zinnias are tender annuals that have been a garden standby for generations. Maybe that's because they fill out so nicely and make such great cut flowers. They grow to some 30" in height and feature clusters of bright, cheerful flowers. Bonus: most zinnias are long-flowering—they bloom all summer.

• Zinnias like full sun and moist to dry soil.

• To plant, dig a hole large enough to hold plant roots. Space 4" to 18" apart. Water thoroughly after planting, then twice a week throughout the growing season.

ANNUALS SOURCES

Gurney's Seed
& Nursery Co. 605-665-1671

Park Seed
Company 800-845-3369

Thompson
& Morgan 800-274-7333

W. Atlee
Burpee Co. 800-888-1447

BULBS

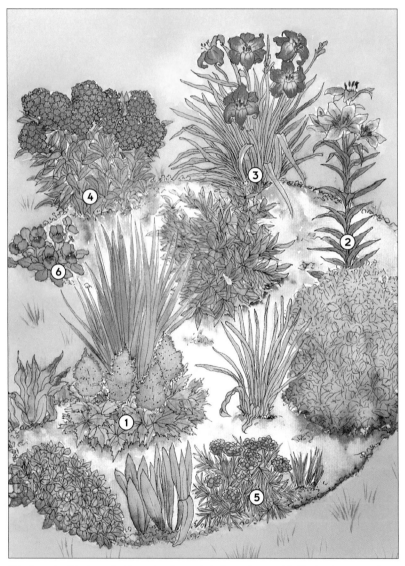

This flower bed is planted with a mix of annuals, bulbs, and perennials for three seasons of color. In summer: 1) astilbe, 2) lily, 3) daylily, and 4) phlox will all come into bloom. And annuals like 5) marigold and 6) pansy will spread and continue flowering. The same bed can be planted so that it will continue blooming in fall (see page 118).

Get ready to be amazed. Some plants have the ability to store the food they need in a neat little package known as a bulb. Once planted, these bulbs use the stored food to grow roots and, come spring, send up gorgeous flowers. It's a bit like the caterpillar's cocoon opening up to release a butterfly. You've heard of daffodils? Tulips? Lilies? These favorites, and others (see box on page 115), are all bulbs. Bonus: most bulbs will come back each spring for two to five years. Some will come back forever.

Hold on; before you start shopping, you need to know a little botany. There are several types of plants lumped into the category nursery people call bulbs. First real *bulbs*—these are bud-shaped guys; then *corms*—they resemble slightly flattened bulbs on the outside but have a different inside. Both bulbs and corms should be planted 2" to 8" deep, pointed-end up. *Tubers* and *rhizomes* look more like fat roots. They are planted close to the surface. *Tuber-corms* are disk-shaped bulbs and are planted like bulbs.

Bulbs are sold in plastic bags (usually singly or by the dozen) in garden centers or by mail-order catalogs. You want large, firm bulbs that have no mold. As with annuals, a bulb's ability to deal with cold weather (called hardiness) is a factor in what to buy. You may have more success with the hardy bulbs. Spring-flowering bulbs should be planted in the fall; those that flower in the summer, like lilies, should be planted in spring. If you buy bulbs early, store them in a dark, cool place (basement or closet) until you are ready to plant.

These crocuses will flower even through snow.

Yellow and white daffodils 1) bloom after crocuses.

CROCUS

These cheerful, superhardy corms are often the first flowers of spring. Their short-stalked flowers range in height from 4" to 6" and come in colors of white, yellow, lilac, and deep purple. Because they are so low to the ground, they stand out nicely between tree roots, along a pathway, or in the lawn.

• To plant, dig holes 3" deep in a sunny spot; space 4" apart. For a more colorful effect, group a number of corms together, four to a large hole. Water well after planting.

• Blooms in early spring.

DAFFODIL

Another favorite bulb, the hardy daffodil grows 12" to 18" in height and blooms in stunning shades of yellow and white. Some varieties have pink or orange centers. Plant along a walkway or the edge of a line of trees.

• To plant, dig a hole 8" deep in a sunny or lightly shaded spot. Space bulbs 6" to 10" apart. Water well.

• Blooms in early to late spring, depending on the variety.

OTHER HARDY BULBS
Grape hyacinth
Grecian windflower
Siberian squill
Snowdrop
Spanish bluebell

BULBS CONT'D

Jonquils are fragrant, unlike their larger cousins, daffodils. Plant them near the deck or patio, where their scent will be appreciated.

HYACINTH

This hardy bulb with extremely fragrant rows of bell-shaped blooms ranges in height from 8" to 12" and comes in myriad colors, most commonly blue, white, and pink. It makes a nice addition to a flower bed.

• To plant, dig a hole 6" deep in a sunny spot. Space bulbs 6" to 10" apart. Water well after planting.

• Blooms in spring.

JONQUIL

Jonquils look like little daffodils but have smaller, very fragrant flowers. Although they look dainty, they are just as hardy as daffodils. Jonquils grow 8" to 16" tall. Plant in window boxes or where you would a daffodil.

• To plant, dig a hole 6" deep in a sunny spot. Space bulbs 4" to 6" apart. Water well.

• Blooms from early to late spring.

FORCING BULBS

"Forcing" a bulb means making it flower (forcing) at a time other than it would naturally. Tulips, daffodils, hyacinths, crocuses, and especially paper-whites (a type of daffodil) all respond well to forcing. Buy bulbs from your local nursery in the fall. Plant immediately or store in your refrigerator until you are ready. Simply: 1) Press the bulbs—wide-end down—into a pot of gravel or commercial potting mix. 2) Water well and 3) put the pot in a garage or other cool, dark area (where it's protected from mice). 4) Lightly water the pot every week. 5) After sprouts appear, in two or three months, move the pot to a dimly lit, cool place for one week, then to a sunny spot.

The lily is tall and its flowers are showy and often fragrant, making them ideal cutting flowers.

LILY

This hardy bulb comes in more than 80 species and even more varieties, ranging in height from 3' to 5'. The standard bloom is trumpet-shaped and is available in many colors, from the spotted ORANGE TIGER to the stunning white EASTER LILY. These tall beauties are great in flower beds and along a fence.

• To plant, dig a hole 6" to 8" deep in a sunny spot. Water well.

• Blooms in summer.

SHORTCUTS • For an extended season of bloom, buy a mix of early-, mid-, and late-season bulbs. Plant them together in the fall and they will bloom in succession in the spring.

Tulips come in a vast array of colors, shapes, and forms, including double, ruffled, and even lily shaped.

PLANT SMART

PLANT	HEIGHT	ZONE
Crocus	4"–6"	
Daffodil	12"–18"	
Hyacinth	8"–12"	
Jonquil	8"–16"	
Lily	3'–5'	
Tulip	6"–24"	

TULIP

There are thousands of tulip varieties out there, making this hardy bulb the queen of bulbs. The standard tulip ranges in height from 6" to 24" and comes in all colors of the rainbow—even black.

• To plant, dig a hole 6" to 8" deep in a sunny spot. Or group a number of bulbs together, four to a large hole. Water well.

• Blooms in spring.

TROUBLE • Nothing came up in the spring? 1) Bulbs weren't hardy for your zone. 2) Bulbs were planted too shallow—plant deeper next year. Or 3) critters ate them. Next time spray bulb with animal repellent (ask your local nursery about it) or plant bulbs inside a wire mesh cage anchored with a few rocks.

BULB SOURCES

Breck's
Dutch Bulbs 800-722-9069

The Daffodil Mart . 800-255-2852

Dutch Gardens 800-775-2852

John Scheepers 860-567-0838

Van Bourgondien's . 800-622-9959

Van Dyck's 800-248-2852

PERENNIALS

With perennials (flowering plants that bloom every year), you've hit the big time. Perennials can bloom in spring, summer, or fall, depending on the plant and your climate. Come winter, the plants "die back," meaning the leaves and stems fall off at ground level. Then in spring the growth process starts all over again.

Perennials are most commonly sold in plastic containers but are sometimes sold bare-root through the mail. To plant see the Smart Guide on page 108. To avoid heartache check your zone before you buy. Also check out your soil—most perennials do well in average soil (not too dry or too moist). Pay attention to placement—most perennials require sun, although some can get by with partial sun. Note: Perennials become fully established and vigorous two to three years after planting.

Most perennials remain in bloom for a few weeks. If you want to extend the blooming season, practice something called "deadheading," snipping or pinching off dead flowers. This tells the plant to send up another flower. Come late fall, remove any dead flowers or foliage. After the first real freeze, cut the stems to the ground (yep, to the ground). Don't worry, they'll come back—and stronger.

This flower bed is planted with a mix of annuals, bulbs, and perennials for three seasons of color. In fall, the following will bloom: first 1) aster. Continuing to bloom will be 2) phlox, 3) astilbe, and 4) daylily. And annual 5) pansy and 6) marigold will still bloom until frost. By or before the first frost, cut back the entire flower bed to a few inches above the ground.

Astilbes like the shade. Their feathery flowers last a long time and will brighten shady spots. Bonus: their glossy, fernlike leaves look great all season long.

ASTER

Don't be confused—some asters are also known as Michaelmas daisies. Asters grow from 8" all the way up to 7' high, and their flowers come in white, red, pink, blue, and purple. Depending on your climate zone, asters bloom from June through October. Plant in flower beds.

• Asters grow best in full sun in average soil. Space 1' to 2' apart. Plant in either spring or fall. Stake tall types so that they don't fall over. Cut plants to ground level when flowering is over. Water thoroughly after planting, then during any dry spells.

• Blooms in late summer and fall.

ASTILBE

Astilbes are the perfect perennials for shady places. There are lots of different kinds, from short ones 1' tall to those more than 3' high. They all have dark green leaves and powder-puff flower plumes in white, pink, rosy purple, or red.

• Astilbes grow best in partial shade, in fertile, moist soil. Space plants 12" to 18" apart and fertilize in spring. Water thoroughly after planting and then during dry spells.

• Blooms in late summer and fall.

New England asters will continue to flower through the first frost.

PERENNIALS CONT'D

Chrysanthemums perk up fall gardens just when other flowers run out of steam. Some people treat them like annuals, buying some each year to fill bare spots in flower beds or replace spent annuals.

CHRYSAN-THEMUM

Technically, chrysanthemums—or mums, as they are called in the trade—are daisies. Mums range in height from 1' to 3'. The popular florist chrysanthemum has large pom-pom–like flowers that come in rich fall colors: the classic gold, burgundy, dusty pink, and white. Plant in flower beds.

• Chrysanthemums grow best in moist, well-drained soil in full sun or light shade. Plant in late summer or early fall and space 2' to 3' apart. Water thoroughly after planting, then during dry spells; fertilize lightly in summer.

• Blooms in fall. Remove dead flowers to encourage new blooms. After flowering, cut back to 6" above the ground.

DAISY

There are more than 200 types of daisies out there, and they bloom at different times. The favorite white-petaled, yellow-centered daisy blooms in summer. It grows from 1' to 3' in height. Plant in flower beds.

• Daisies grow best in moist, well-drained soil in full sun. Plant in spring and space 12" to 18" apart. Water thoroughly after planting, then during any dry spells.

• Blooms in summer. In late fall, trim plants to the ground. Tall varieties (such as 'ALASKA' and 'MOUNT SHASTA') may need staking.

Daisies add an informal note to beds and bouquets. Here, 1) golden marguerites pair with 2) classic white shastas.

DAYLILY

Daylilies are some of the easiest flowers to grow. They're also some of the most beautiful, with trumpet-shaped flowers in shades of white, yellow, orange, or red. There are even some that bloom just about all summer long.

- Daylilies do best in average soil in full sun to light shade. Space plants 12" to 18" apart in spring or fall. Just plant, water thoroughly, and let grow.

- Blooms from early summer to early fall.

Forget-me-nots are ideal for small places, such as window boxes and pond banks.

Daylilies come in a wide variety of colors and are the ultimate easy-care flowers.

FORGET-ME-NOT

This pretty little creeping plant comes in both annual and perennial forms. Forget-me-nots reach 12" to 18" in height, making them ideal as edging plants.

- Forget-me-nots like moist, well-drained soil and partial shade. They will grow in full sun if soil is very moist. Plant in spring or fall; dig a hole large enough to hold plant roots. Space 12" apart and water well after planting.

- Blooms in spring and summer.

TROUBLE

- Tall plants flopping over? Stake them when you plant with circular wire supports. Stems will grow through the hoop and quickly hide the support.

- Perennials producing fewer flowers? Dig up and divide plants every 3 to 4 years to keep them growing strong (see page 108).

- White spots on leaves? It's mildew, probably caused by overcrowding and poor air circulation. Spray affected plants with a fungicide (see page 38). Next spring, divide plants to relieve over-crowding.

PERENNIALS CONT'D

Irises look best if planted in clumps of the same color.

These perennial geraniums, called cranesbills like partial sun and spread quickly.

GERANIUMS

Geraniums are quite different from the annual plants that are called by the same name. These beauties grow from 6" to 3' high and are covered with white, pink, lilac-blue, or magenta flowers in spring and summer. Geraniums are pretty in flower beds, and some make nice ground covers. (The annual geranium is only distantly related; it offers up big balls of flowers in bright red, white, or pink and does well in containers.)

• Geraniums like moist, well-drained soil and full sun to shade. Plant in spring or fall. To plant, dig a hole large enough to hold plant roots. Space 12" to 24" apart. Water well.

• Blooms in summer.

IRIS

This pretty perennial comes in a variety of flower sizes, colors, and heights (CRESTED IRIS reaches 8"; the SIBERIAN IRIS grows as high as 3'.) Then there are the petals—the bold flowers of the BEARDED IRIS bloom in late spring, and the more delicate JAPANESE IRIS blooms in early summer. One thing they all share: beautiful blooms—in colors ranging from white, yellow, and pink to purple. Plant in flower beds or borders. WATER IRISES like to be planted near ponds.

• Soil and sun needs depend upon the variety of iris you've chosen. Read the nursery tag carefully. Same goes for spacing. Plant bearded irises in fall, others in spring or fall.

• Blooms from spring to summer. Remove dead flowers to encourage more blooms. In late fall, trim down to just above the ground.

PHLOX ◗ ◗ ◗ ◗

Garden phlox is popular for its bright colors and fragrant flowers. (*Phlox* is Greek for "flame.") The five-petaled flowers come in red, orange, pink, white, and violet and are ideal for cut flowers. The plant reaches 4' and is good for the rear of a flower bed or border.

• Phlox needs moist, well-drained soil and full sun. Plant in spring or fall and space 18" to 24" apart. Water thoroughly.

• Blooms midsummer to fall. Remove dead flowers to encourage more blooms. In late fall trim plants back to the ground.

Peonies 1) are low-maintenance roses—just as showy and fragrant but requiring little work.

PEONY ◗ ◗ ◗ ◗

The common peony offers up huge 4" to 8", round flowers ranging in color from white, red, peach, and yellow to pink. Each spring the plant grows into a dense 3'-tall bush. The blooms are so huge that peonies need to be staked. Peonies make pretty plantings in front of foundations or in a flower bed.

• Peonies like moist soil and sun to light shade. Plant in spring or fall. Space 2½' to 3' apart, water thoroughly, and stake.

• Blooms in spring. Remove dead flowers. In the fall trim plants back to the ground.

Phlox 1) is a late-season bloomer, adding color to fall gardens.

PLANT SMART

FLOWERS	HEIGHT	ZONE
Aster	8"–84"	◗ ◗ ◗
Astilbe	1'–3'	◗ ◗ ◗
Chrysanthemum	1'–3'	◗ ◗ ◗
Daisy	1'–3'	◗ ◗ ◗
Daylily	1½'–6'	◗ ◗ ◗ ◗
Forget-me-not	12"–18"	◗ ◗
Geranium	6"–36"	◗ ◗ ◗
Iris	6"–36"	◗ ◗ ◗
Peony	3'	◗ ◗ ◗
Phlox	4'	◗ ◗ ◗ ◗

PERENNIALS SOURCES

Gilbert H.
Wild & Son LLC . . . 417-548-3514

Klehm Nursery. 800-553-3715

Schreiners
Gardens 800-525-2367

Spring Hill Nurseries 800-582-8527

Wayside Gardens. . . 800-845-1124

White Flower Farm . 800-503-9624

SPECIALTY GARDENS

Use them to add a little fun to your yard or to solve problems—such as serious shade or rocky slopes. Start small and see what works best for your yard. Read on to discover how easy it is to begin.

SMART GUIDE 126/127

WATER GARDENS 128/129

ROCK GARDENS 130/131

ROSE GARDENS 132/133

CONTAINER GARDENS . . . 134/135

KITCHEN GARDENS 136/137

CHILDREN'S GARDENS . . . 138/139

SPECIALTY GARDENS

To get specialty garden smart, use this easy number guide to identify and site a specialty garden. Detailed explanations of siting and creating these gardens follow in this chapter.

WATER GARDEN

1 . . . PLACE AT YARD BORDER

2 . . . SUBMERGED PREFORMED PLASTIC SHELL

3 . . . PLANT DEEP WATER PLANTS (not shown)

4 . . . SHALLOW-WATER PLANTS

ROCK GARDEN

5 . . . PLACE AT YARD BORDER

6 . . . MIX OF VARIOUS-SIZED ROCKS

7 . . . GROUND COVER

ROSE GARDEN

8 . . . PLANT IN FULL SUN (6 hours)

9 . . . MULCH

CONTAINER GARDEN

10 . . . PLACE ON DECK AND OR TO COVER BARE SPOTS IN GARDEN

11 . . . PUT FRAGRANT PLANTS NEAR SITTING AREA

KITCHEN GARDEN

12 . . . PLANT IN FULL TO PARTIAL SUN

13 . . . ROWS FOR FOOTPATHS

14 . . . RICH, FERTILIZED SOIL

CHILDREN'S GARDEN

15 . . . SITE SO VISIBLE FROM HOUSE

16 . . . PLACE IN FULL SUN

17 . . . NEAR CHILDREN'S PLAY AREA (playhouse and sandbox)

18 . . . NECTAR-PRODUCING PLANTS (to attract birds and butterflies)

WATER GARDENS

A water garden can be tucked in almost any-where. After adding water plants, such as 1) water lilies, soften the edge of the pond with other plants, such as 2) zinnias and 3) dwarf pittosporum.

It's easier than you think, honest. You can start small with a half barrel or a large preformed plastic shell or, for a more natural shape, plastic liners that you cut to the size and shape you want. The point is to use water to create a tranquil focal point in your yard. And, of course, to plant wonderfully lush water plants. You don't need an estate, just a sunny spot. How sunny? Most aquatic plants need six hours of full sun a day.

But first, a little botany. There are three types of water plants: 1) *Deep-water* plants (WATER LILY); plant these in pots and submerge them. 2) *Shallow-water* plants (YELLOW FLAG, LOTUS); these are also planted in containers and sunk below the surface but need only about 6" of water. Place on a brick or upside-down pot to get the right height, or set on the shelf of a preformed shell. 3) *Floaters* (WATER LETTUCE), which float freely atop the water.

If you want fish, you'll need a pond that is at least 50 sq. ft. and 18" to 24" deep. That's big. Hire help to excavate the hole. Add plants called *oxygenators* (EEL GRASS, WATER MILFOIL) to create a healthy environment for fish. Bonus: these plants will help keep your pond free of algae.

Any large, watertight container like this tub can become a water garden.

The summer blooms of water lilies are the stars of any water garden.

Want moving water? You'll need a pump, a slope, flexible pipe, and a good design. Here, a flexible liner keeps the water in the streambed, which can include rocks, waterfalls, and pools. Water is pumped from the bottom, through the pipe, back to the top.

TROUBLE

• Zoning problems? Some towns have the same zoning requirements for ponds as for pools. Check before you dig.

• Liability? Any attraction in your yard (pools, ponds) should be fenced to protect children and animals from harm.

WATER-GARDEN RESOURCES

Lilypons Water
Gardens 800-999-5459

Little Giant Pump
Company 405-947-2511

Paradise Water
Gardens Ltd. 800-955-0161

Perry's Water
Gardens 704-524-3264

Slocum Water
Gardens 941-293-7151

SHORTCUTS
• All water-garden plants, except floaters, need to be planted in plastic pots with holes in the bottom or side. (Line with burlap if holes are too big.) Place a layer of gravel on top of the pot's soil to keep soil inside the pot.

• Water lilies may be hardy or tropical. Hardy varieties can survive winter if the pond does not freeze. Tropical water lilies need to be replaced every year, except in frost-free regions.

• To keep fish, install a water pump or fountain to circulate and oxygenate the water. All pump hookups (also filters and lights) should be installed by a licensed electrician and connected to a GFCI (ground fault circuit interrupter) receptacle to prevent electrical shock.

PLANT SMART

PLANT	TYPE	ZONE
Eel grass	Oxygenator	🍃 🍃 🍃 🍃
Lotus	Shallow-water	🍃 🍃 🍃 🍃
Water lettuce	Floater	🍃 🍃
Water lily	Deep-water	🍃 🍃 🍃 🍃
Water milfoil	Oxygenator	🍃 🍃 🍃 🍃
Yellow flag	Shallow-water	🍃

ROCK GARDENS

Turn a rocky slope into a stunning rock garden. Mix mound-forming perennials, such as 1) inula and 2) dianthus; ground covers, such as 3) bearberry; and 4) dwarf evergreens.

The solution is the same whether your yard is full of rocks or you love stone and wish it were: create a rock garden. A true rock garden resembles a miniature mountainside, with rocks of various sizes and similar colors cascading down a slope. Ideally, you need a mix of one to two boulders, some medium-size rocks, and then small ones to fill in the gaps.

So much for the rock—what about the garden? Most rock-garden plants thrive in average or even poor soil, and, once they've grown in, these gardens need little or no water, fertilizer, or weed-ing. It's smart to plant a mix of perennials, either spreading or mounded.

Rock gardens work best in sunny spots. Start with such perennials as BASKET-OF-GOLD, CANDYTUFT, CREEPING VERONICA, PURPLE ROCK CRESS, SILVER MOUND ARTEMESIA, and WALL ROCK CRESS. Add spring bulbs and low-growing annuals to provide lots of color. You can also include flowering ground covers like the creeping thymes and sedums (see page 60). Rock gardens will work in partial shade if you choose shade-tolerant plants such as violets, bleeding-heart 'Luxuriant', small varieties of hostas, and green-and-gold.

CREATION AND CARE

✔ For long, sloping rock gardens, arrange stones in a series of ledges to make the garden appear more natural.

✔ Bury one-half to two-thirds of each new rock to give it a natural appearance.

✔ If your rock garden will be viewed from a distance, mass up to a dozen plants of the same color and type.

✔ To put in plants, dig individual pockets for each one. Add extra soil.

TROUBLE

• Disappearing leaves? Suspect caterpillars or slugs. These pests are drawn to rock gardens. Knock out caterpillars with Bt (*Bacillus thuringiensis*, a natural insecticide); get it and slug traps at your local garden center.

• Rotten plants? Remove fallen leaves from between rocks or they'll form a wet mat, suffocating the poor little plants underneath.

• Plants died over winter? Improve drainage by mixing sand or fine gravel into soil before putting in new plants. In late fall, cover plants with several inches of loose straw.

For a simple rock garden, place larger rocks as you wish and add a couple of inches of gravel or small stones, and plants. Here, a simple but pleasing arrangement is made of dianthus, both 1) in flower and 2) just past blooming, along with 3) coralbells, 4) tunic flower, and 5) edelweiss.

PLANT SMART

PLANT	HEIGHT	ZONE
Basket-of-gold	6"–8"	
Candytuft	6"	
Creeping veronica	3"–8"	
Purple rock cress	3"–6"	
Silver mound artemesia	6"–8"	
Wall rock cress	6"–10"	

A shallow trough or a crack in a large rock can be made to bloom. Simply add soil and a few plants for an instant mini rock garden. Here, there is 1) red cyclamen, 2) liriope, 3) primrose, and 4) hen-and-chickens.

ROSE GARDENS

Plant roses near entranceways or walkways so that their lovely fragrance can be better enjoyed. Here 'Cécile Brunner' is trained to arch over a rustic gate into the garden.

Thanks to the miracle of hybrids (new plant varieties), you can get roses that bloom for more than just a couple of weeks. If you pick the right one, it will continue to bloom for most of the summer with minimal fuss.

Start your garden by figuring out the right roses for you. Some of the easiest to grow are called varieties or cultivars in the trade. (They have single quotes around their names.) These babies resist diseases and tolerate neglect. Best choices include deep pink 'WILLIAM BAFFIN', golden 'SUNSPRITE', white 'MARGARET MERRIL', crimson 'MORDEN CENTENNIAL', and pale pink 'CÉCILE BRUNNER'. These keep blooming after the main early-summer show, and all but superhardy 'William Baffin' are fragrant.

Roses will reward you if you give them what they need. Pick a spot with at least six hours of direct sun; the more the better! (Morning sun helps prevent diseases by drying dew quickly.) Give roses rich, well-drained soil. Add compost (see page 32) to yours if it's too compact. Putting mulch (see page 32) around roses helps keep weeds down and reduces watering chores. (Bonus: mulches improve soil as they break down.) Roses also like some fertilizer to create the best blooms.

BUYING, PLANTING, AND CARE

✔ Plant roses in early to late spring, before hot weather arrives. Nurseries sell roses in containers. Most mail-order roses are shipped with their bare roots wrapped in sphagnum moss; these must be planted immediately.

✔ Plant roses the same way as decorative shrubs (see Smart Guide, page 94).

✔ Give roses a good soaking once a week, so that 4" to 6" of soil is moist, to encourage roots to grow down deep and help them withstand drought. In sandy soils or during hot, dry spells, water roses every four to five days.

✔ Feed roses with a rose or general garden fertilizer twice a year: in early spring when new plant growth appears and again after the first blooms appear.

✔ Practice deadheading—snipping off the dying flowers—to encourage rosebushes to form new buds.

✔ In late fall cut rose stems back to 3' and pile several inches of mulch around the base.

 TROUBLE

• Spots on leaves? It's probably blackspot, powdery mildew, or rust. You may need a fungicide (see page 38), especially where summers are warm and humid. Prune badly diseased stems to 1" below damaged area.

• Bugs on the buds? Probably aphids. Knock them off with a good shot of water from the garden hose. Repeat every few days for two weeks to make sure you get them all.

PLANT SMART

PLANT	HEIGHT	ZONE		
'Cécile Brunner'	2'		🍃 🍃 🍃
'Margaret Merril'	3'-4'	🍃	🍃 🍃 🍃
'Morden Centennial'	4'	🍃	🍃 🍃 🍃
'Sunsprite'	4'		🍃 🍃 🍃
'William Baffin'	8'	🍃	🍃 🍃 🍃

ROSE RESOURCES

Edmunds Roses . . . 888-481-7673

Heritage Rose
Foundation 919-834-2591

Jackson & Perkins . . 800-872-7673

The Roseraie
at Bayfields 207-832-6330

Whiting Nursery . . . 707-963-5358

'Margaret Merril'

'Sunsprite'

'Morden Centennial'

'William Baffin'

CONTAINER GARDENS

Mass many containers of individual plants to create a dramatic display. Rotate pots when one plant is not blooming. Here the color comes from 1) pansies, 2) geraniums, 3) sedums, 4) petunias, and 5) parsley.

By using various-size containers, you can create a whole garden regardless of your yard's soil or amount of light. Plus, you can move and rearrange your containers—even bring them indoors—whenever you want.

And containers are so easy to plant. Some simple rules: 1) Pick a pot. Just about any type of container can be used, as long as it has one or more holes to let water drain out. Try classic terra-cotta (or plastic look-alikes), wooden half barrels, strawberry jars, and those "special" tag-sale finds. 2) Cover drainage holes with a few pieces of gravel, shards of broken terra-cotta

pots, or a piece of screen. 3) Fill pot with potting soil (available at any garden center or nursery). Potting soil is not really soil but an ingenious mix of peat moss and other substances that holds water and allows enough air for drainage. Because these mixes don't have lots of natural nutrients, you should 4) add fertilizer. 5) Water immediately after planting to settle soil around roots. Note: Plants in pots dry out much more quickly than those in the ground, so check the soil daily. If dry, water so 1" of topsoil is wet.

Fill pots with annuals for the easiest container garden. Annuals grow quickly and bloom longer than perennials.

Window boxes are heavy and need to be attached securely to the side of the house with sturdy brackets.

If you use a wire basket as a container, you'll have to line it. Try sphagnum moss or coconut fiber (sold at most nurseries). Or ask your nursery to line it and fill it with soil—some will for a small charge.

SHORTCUTS • If a container will be viewed from one side, plant the shorties in the front and tall guys in back. Containers viewed from all angles should have the tallest plants in the center, with shorter varieties grouped around them.

• Wooden boxes make great planters; just drill a few drainage holes in the bottom and elevate off the ground so the wood won't rot. A caster screwed at each corner—or a purchased tray with wheels—makes it easy to roll large planters around.

TROUBLE • Got little kids? Some plants are toxic if eaten. Plant child-safe plants if you plan to bring your containers indoors for the winter. Display plants where they are out of the reach of small children.

• Plants looking lopsided? Give each container a half turn weekly to encourage even growth in all directions.

• Flowers flagging? Your plant needs fertilizer. Get a slow-release fertilizer; you can apply a spoonful once or twice while the plants are growing and not worry about it again.

• Frost killed your potted plants? This is natural. Annuals die when hit by cold weather. Empty pots, wash with a scrub brush, and store until spring, when you replant with new annuals.

PLANT SMART

PLANT	HEIGHT	ZONE			
Chrysanthemum	1'–3'	🍃	🍃	🍃	🍃
Geranium	6"–24"	🍃	🍃	🍃	🍃
Marigold	6"–36"	🍃	🍃	🍃	🍃
Pansy	6"–9"	🍃	🍃	🍃	🍃
Petunia	10"–24"	🍃	🍃	🍃	🍃

CONTAINER SOURCES

Al's Garden Art. . . . 909-424-0221

Garden
Crafter's, Inc. 212-966-6030

Gardeners Eden. . . . 800-822-1214

Gardener's Supply
Company 800-876-5520

Kinsman Company . 800-733-4146

Rowe Pottery
Works 800-356-5003

KITCHEN GARDENS

Before you plant, draw your garden with crop selections on paper. This will help you avoid overcrowding. Try mixing 1) red and green leaf lettuce, 2) parsley, 3) peas, and 4) carrots.

It's true: no vegetables or herbs taste fresher than those you grow yourself. Even a tiny garden can yield a satisfying amount of produce, so roll up your sleeves and dive in. A 15' x 20' garden can easily provide enough vegetables for a family of four.

To thrive, most vegetables and herbs need two things: full sun and rich soil. Full sun means at least six hours per day (LEAF LETTUCE and PARSLEY put up with a little less). Rich soil is dark, crumbly, and easily forms into a ball when moist. Less-than-ideal soil? Add lots of compost or well-aged manure before you fertilize (you can buy these in 25- and 50-pound bags). Or, if you want to get gardening right away, hammer together a raised bed or two out of scrap lumber and fill with purchased topsoil.

Some herbs and vegetables, like CUCUMBER, should be started right in the ground. Others, like lettuce, parsley, OREGANO, and BASIL, as well as TOMATO, react well to transplanting; buy them as seedlings at your local garden center or start them indoors in trays, under artificial light.

SHORTCUTS

• Locate your kitchen garden close to the house. It will be more convenient to pick the plants—and, if you can see it, you're more likely to weed and water!

• To avoid an overload of fast-growing lettuce, plant small crops every two or three weeks until early summer. When you're finished eating one harvest, the next will be ready.

• Tomatoes and basil can't take frost. Plant seedlings only after you're sure the last threat of frost has passed. (Late in the season, throw an old sheet over these plants any night that frost is expected.)

• Don't crowd your vegetables. Check when planting seedlings to see how far apart they need to be—usually 8" to 12".

• Rotate location of plants every year to improve soil and avoid diseases.

TROUBLE

• Hungry critters? Unfortunately, there's no foolproof way to stop woodchucks, deer, and rabbits from eating your vegetables before you do. Milorganite, an organic fertilizer, is said to repel animals, but it must be reapplied after every rainfall. You may have to put up a fence; otherwise, plant extras so there's some left for you!

• Short on space? Grow herbs and vegetables in containers (see page 134). Put one dwarf cucumber or dwarf tomato plant in a 12" container. Plant three lettuce, basil, oregano, or parsley plants in a 12" pot.

Plant in pots if you have nowhere else to put a kitchen garden. Here a 1) dwarf tomato plant mixes with 2) peppers, 3) parsley, 4) strawberries, and 5) pink and white forms of decorative sweet alyssum for a tiny container garden.

PLANT SMART

PLANT	ZONE
Basil	🍃 🍃 🍃 🍃
Cucumber	🍃 🍃 🍃 🍃
Lettuce	🍃 🍃 🍃 🍃
Oregano	🍃 🍃 🍃
Parsley	🍃 🍃 🍃 🍃
Tomato	🍃 🍃 🍃 🍃

SEED SOURCES

DeGiorgi Seeds
& Goods 800-858-2580

Gilbertie's Herbs . . . 203-227-4175

Gurney's Seed &
Nursery Co. 605-665-1671

Johnny's
Selected Seeds 207-437-4357

Park Seed
Company 800-845-3369

Stokes Seeds, Inc. . . . 716-695-6980

CHILDREN'S GARDENS

Build a simple tepee with wooden poles and start pole beans around it. As the beans grow up the tepee, it will become a hideout for kids.

Planting and tending a garden gives children more than a firsthand experience of the wonders of nature. It can teach them how to think and plan. Figure out together what to plant; if you let children decide what to grow, they're more likely to stay interested. Pique their interest and suggest theme gardens, such as a "pizza garden" of tomatoes, peppers, oregano, and basil. Does the name "lamb's-ears" tickle your child's funny bone? Then let him or her grow them. Is pink a favorite color? Try an all-pink flower garden.

Now for the gentle art of planning. Start by having the kids draw their gar-den. Figure out how many of each plant they'll need for the amount of space they have. Start some seeds indoors and watch plants grow toward the artificial lights. Think of it as fun science. Start small, by setting aside a corner of your own garden or by planting a simple container. As children mature, their gardens can grow with them.

If your children are too young to sow their own seeds, try a garden that appeals to hummingbirds and butter-flies. Plant lots of nectar-producing plants, such as the perennials BEE BALM, JUPITER'S BEARD, JOE-PYE WEED, BUTTERFLY BUSH, and PURPLE CONEFLOWER.

HELPFUL HINTS

CHECKLIST ✔Buy work gloves and a set of kid-size tools for your gardener. Gloves prevent blisters, and the smaller handles on kids' tools are easier to grip than those on models for grown-ups.

✔Children under five find big seeds easiest to plant. Try squash, sunflower, pea, and bean seeds.

✔The small varieties of vegetables bred especially for containers are particularly appealing to kids. (Dwarf sunflowers have the same charm.) Try growing bush cukes and patio-type tomatoes either in part of your regular garden or in a large pot or half barrel. Kids like container gardens because they're small and manageable.

✔Teach your children to water deeply. Also show them how to weed; tell them that plants need to be taken care of, just like pets.

✔Purchase a pint-size wheelbarrow or red wagon. They're fun for hauling around soil, watering cans, and the harvest.

PLANT SMART

PLANT	HEIGHT	ZONE			
Bee balm	3'–4'	●	●	●	●
Butterfly bush	3'–15'	●	●	●	
Joe-Pye weed	2'–9'	●	●	●	
Jupiter's beard	2'–3'	●	●	●	
Purple coneflower	3'	●	●	●	
Trumpet creeper	to 40'		●	●	

FLOWERS THAT ATTRACT WILDLIFE

Attracting wildlife like butterflies, birds, and hummingbirds to a child's garden is simple. Just plant any of the following plants. But be warned: anything that attracts hummingbirds will also attract bees, which are fascinating to watch but can sting.

Butterfly bush provides nectar for a tiger swallowtail butterfly.

Bee balm does indeed attract bees.

Joe-Pye weed with a monarch butterfly.

Jupiter's beard feeds birds and butterflies over a long season.

Purple coneflower hosts a great spangled fritillary butterfly.

Trumpet creeper blossoms are a favorite of hummingbirds.

KIDS' GARDEN RESOURCES

Aquapore Moisture Systems, Inc.. . . 800-635-8379
Ferry Morse Seed Company 800-283-3400
Lee Valley Tools Ltd. 800-871-8158
Shepherd's Garden Seeds 860-482-3638
Union Tools 614-222-4476

PATIOS/ DECKS/ POOLS

FENCES 144/145

STONE WALLS 146/147

PERGOLAS/ARBORS/TRELLISES ...148/149

PATIOS 150/151

DECKS 152/153

POOLS 154/155

KIDS' PLAY AREAS 156/157

SHEDS 158/159

YARD SAFETY 160/161

L andscape professionals refer to patios, decks, pools, and other such man-made wonders as "hardscape." The goal is to blend these backyard assets with nature. Read on and learn how.

PATIOS/ DECKS/POOLS

These man-made features add to the enjoyment of your home and to the value of your house. Use this easy number guide to identify the features you want. Detailed explanations follow in this chapter.

FENCES

1 . . . PRIVACY FENCE (6' high)

2 . . . SAFETY FENCE AROUND POOL

3 . . . SELF-LATCHING GATE

STONE WALLS

4 . . . FREESTANDING STONE WALL

5 . . . FLAGSTONE WALKWAY

PERGOLAS/ARBORS/TRELLISES

6 . . . ARBOR

7 . . . TRELLIS FOR CLIMBING PLANTS

DECK

8 . . . PRESSURE-TREATED WOOD

9 . . . HANDRAIL

PATIO

10 . . . FLAGSTONE PATIO

POOL

11 . . . IN-GROUND POOL

12 . . . DIVING BOARD

KIDS' PLAY AREA

13 . . . CHILDREN'S GARDEN

14 . . . PLAYHOUSE

SHEDS

15 . . . POOL/GARDEN SHED

16 . . . LOCKED DOOR

17 . . . WINDOW FOR INTERIOR LIGHTING

FENCES

A low fence keeps kids and pets safe without seeming to confine the area. To create an open feel, try see-through styles like this redwood fence complete with driveway gate.

Want privacy, shelter from wind, and security for children and pets? Add a fence. It can also separate areas of your yard for different uses or mark property borders.

Two rules about fences: 1) Some towns have ordinances about how high fences can be; the standard is no higher than 6' (some homeowners' associations stipulate that fences must meet the homeowners association's approval); 2) if you're putting up the fence, the nice side should face your neighbor.

Now think about style. Fences in urban settings tend to be more ornamental than those in rural or suburban areas, so cruise your neighborhood before you build—if you want to fit in. Next, consider what the fence is for. Privacy? Go for a 6'-high stockade fence. Decorative border marker? Consider a 4'-high picket or lattice fence that sets off your property without blocking your view. A windscreen? Try a stockade fence, hedge (see page 81) or stone wall (see page 146).

Don't forget the gate. Get top-quality hinges and openers to withstand heavy wear. Match the gate and fencing materials or opt for a custom design.

FENCE SMART

✔ Check your local building codes before you have your fence installed. Note: You may need a permit. Determine the location of power and water lines.

✔ Wooden fences can be left to weather if they are made of pressure-treated lumber. If not, you must stain and seal or prime and paint them. Note: Rot-resistant wood, such as cedar, locust, cypress, and redwood, does not need to be stained or painted.

✔ For a painted wood fence, pretreat lumber with primer before the fence goes up; then apply the paint coat.

✔ Ironwork fences must be painted with rust-preventing paint before being installed; repaint every three years.

✔ Make sure your fence lasts longer than a year and a half. Any fence more than 4' tall should have its posts set in concrete or in earth-and-gravel fill if you live in a warm climate where the ground doesn't freeze.

• Did your neighbor give you the ugly side of the fence? Dress up dull surfaces with a reed or bamboo screen, or grow climbing vines. Another option is to install a trellis next to the fence and grow roses or climbing hydrangeas (see page 96).

FENCING SOURCES

Bufftech, Inc. .716-685-1600

Enviroedge Products Company 800-549-3343

Moultrie Manufacturing Company . . .800-841-8674

The Thompson's Company 800-367-6297

Vintage Wood Products 707-585-1717

The classic picket fence serves as a better people barrier than pet barrier. But the gaps between pickets allow plenty of light through, which makes them ideal for flowers.

Sturdy fences make excellent supports for many climbing plants, such as these clematis (see page 104).

STONE WALLS

S tone walls around a house help set it off, much as a jewel is set off by a handsome setting. While they are more expensive to erect than a fence is, stone walls last longer and are maintenance-free.

Walls are built to be freestanding or to retain the earth (that's a retaining wall). The stones in the wall can be dry-stacked or mortared together. Either style can be used when making a retaining wall. To keep back the earth, the stones are stepped back into the slope (this is called battered). If the wall is mortared, it may have small, inconspicuous plastic pipes fitted into its bottom part to allow for drainage. The spaces in dry-stacked walls naturally allow for drainage.

The color and texture of stone vary from region to region. You can find rough fieldstones on the ground just about anywhere. To make a short, dry wall, simply stack them. Quarried stone offers a variety of shapes and sizes, from the straight-line patterns of ashlar stone to the boxy look of limestone and sandstone.

Stones actually comes in a range of colors. Gray is popular, but how about the rust, tan, and blue hues of some sedimentary stone? Yellowish sandstone reflects light. Check quarries in your area to see what's available.

This simple but elegant 3'-high stone retaining wall helps eliminate the slope of the front yard while serving to separate the yard from the sidewalk.

A retaining wall made of stone can be both decorative and functional.

 • Wall falling down?
Unmortared walls are more likely to crumble than mortared ones. Have stone setter reset wall with mortar.

• Tall stone wall look too plain? Add a lower wall a few feet in front, and fill the space with soil to create a cutting garden of annuals or space for bulbs.

STONE SOURCES

Halquist
Stone Company 414-246-3561

Krukowski
Stone Co., Inc.. 715-693-6300

Oldcastle Homecenter
Group 888-450-4114

Rauch Clay
Sales Corp. 773-254-0775

Rocks, Etc.,Inc.. 815-836-0086

 STONE WALL SMART
✔ Ask landscape contractors for the names of stone setters. Get three bids and throw out the lowest. Have a written contract that specifies the type (retaining or freestanding), height, and width of the wall. State the type of stone you want used.

✔ Always look at a sample of the stone before you buy. Walls last a long time, so make sure you like the color and texture.

✔ Specify the range of sizes you want used.

✔ Use fabricated stone to get the look of stone without the expense. Made out of crushed rock and cement, it goes up fast as a facing over concrete blocks.

✔ If you can't afford real or fabricated stone, try using broken concrete. It's usually free, and its craggy look goes with rock-garden plants.

PERGOLAS/ARBORS/TRELLISES

Arbors make elegant passageways. They can support such climbing vines as this pink clematis (see page 104).

Big yards, especially flat ones, often need something to provide a little visual excitement. Enter the gardener's delight: pergolas, arbors, and trellises. These are tall (more than 6' high) structures that are often covered with climbing vines or shrubs.

A *pergola*, essentially a set of posts supporting an open ceiling of widely spaced beams, is easy to install over a deck or patio. Pergolas provide a nice transition between home and garden. Build one over your shed or storage area and it will spiff up the utility areas of your yard. Or put a freestanding one in a quiet area of the yard to create a shady spot. Add a bench.

An *arbor* is an arched support that you can walk through. Put one up to call attention to a pathway from one part of the garden to another. Some have benches built into the sidewall. Choose from wood, brick, metal, or stone. Arbors are ideal supports for climbing vines.

A *trellis* is a flat structure designed solely to support climbing plants. They come in many shapes, from the traditional fan shape to the diamond lattice frame; make sure they are well secured and strong enough to support the plants. Put up a trellis to pretty-up an unattractive fence or wall. Trellises also are at home on the sides of your pergola and arbor.

Pergolas, arbors, and trellises can be custom designed and built, or made from kits. Arbors and trellises can be bought ready-made from most garden and home centers.

For a rustic trellis (above), bend willow branches and tie them together with string. This lightweight trellis can support small vines. A pergola (left) attached to the house, if planted with climbing plants or vining fruits (such as grapes), is a pretty way to provide shade.

 CHECKLIST MATERIALS SMART ✔Choose pergola materials for the look you want to create—fancy stucco columns for a permanent, formal look for outdoor entertaining; rough redwood or cedar or pressure-treated lumber for a casual, weathered look.

✔Set wooden pergola, trellis, and arbor posts in concrete.

PLANT SMART

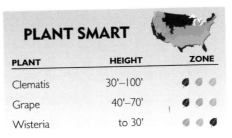

PLANT	HEIGHT	ZONE
Clematis	30'–100'	🍃 🍃 🍃
Grape	40'–70'	🍃 🍃 🍃
Wisteria	to 30'	🍃 🍃 🍃

PERGOLA/ARBOR/ TRELLIS SOURCES

Arboria-
Garden Structures... 503-286-5372

Backyard Products.. 814-455-0074

The Hayes Co., Inc. . 316-838-8000

Island Post Cap 800-767-8227

Newport Garden
Structures 401-849-6850

PATIOS

Patios are set on ground level with the house. The wall around this patio helps set it apart from the yard.

Patios extend your indoor living space to the outdoors. Unlike a deck, a patio is usually set at ground level, offering a comfortable transition between the house and the yard.

Some patio rules of thumb: have the patio area professionally graded. Use the building materials and colors of your house to better complement it. Keep your patio small enough to feel comfortable— a flight deck is no refuge. Add a few small trees and shrubs around the perimeter, to provide shade and a sense of privacy.

Install soft lighting for evenings outside.

The types of paving material and pattern you choose make the patio. Bricks or tile create pattern and texture, which look good in small areas. Larger stones, such as bluestone and fieldstone, are more expensive but give a sophisticated look to big spaces. Concrete comes in endless colors and shapes, from interlocking pavers to cobblestones and imitation "Southwestern" adobe. Pavers and ready-cut concrete are the least-expensive materials. They also last the longest.

Stamped concrete is a less expensive alternative to traditional stone and brick patios. The concrete is poured directly on the graded soil, then the design is pressed into it. It can also be colored.

PATIO-MATERIAL SOURCES

Anderson
Design R. L. 800-947-7697

Berkeley Forge
& Foundry 800-408-0804

Krukowski
Stone Co., Inc. 715-693-6300

Oldcastle Homecenter
Group 888-450-411.4

Rocks, Etc., Inc. 815-836-0086

SHORTCUTS

• Prevent weeds from sprouting between bricks, stone, or concrete pavers set in sand by first laying down "landscape fabric" (available at garden and home centers) under the sand; this will keep weeds down.

• Add a patio wall with built-in planters to provide room to grow flowers, herbs, or even vegetables. Choose fragrant flowers and herbs to add a nice scent to the air.

• If moss is growing in shady areas of patio, scrub it away with a brush and a chlorine-based household cleaner.

TROUBLE

• Patio flooded after a heavy rain? Proper grading at construction time will ensure that excess water is carried away after storms. You may need to start over and regrade the patio area.

• Slippery patio? Flagstone, slate, and ceramic tiles look great, but they can be slick in the rain. Brick or roughened cement provide better footing if you live in a rainy climate.

• Found a stash of salvaged brick? Don't build your patio with it. It may not be intended for outdoor paving and could crumble in freezing temperatures. Buy new brick for the best results.

• Need new patio furniture? If your patio gets a lot of sun, don't buy metal furniture—it will get too hot to sit on. Buy wood.

DECKS

If you build a new house, consider having the deck built at the same time. In the long run, you'll save money by not having to dig up any landscaping work you may have done.

ecks can be built anywhere on your property and at any level—but don't forget you'll need a building permit. A deck can be as simple as a square platform outside the kitchen door or as elaborate as a wraparound, multi-level structure with curved steps.

To get the most from your deck, plan carefully. Think about location first. You'll want easy access from the house and the yard. How much sun or shade do you want on the deck? Factor in the degree of privacy you'll need from the neighbors or the street. Now consider any special features. Do you want a built-in gas grill? Built-in benches or planters? Perhaps a separate area for a spa or a swing? Some of these will require electrical outlets.

Wood decks require maintenance. To protect them from sun and rain, wood decks must be sealed with a deck sealant (a clear varnishlike substance) or with a stain. If you're using pressure-treated wood, wait one year to seal. If you go with cedar, then seal immediately. You will need to reapply a coat of sealant every few years. Decks made of synthetic wood materials require no sealing.

After the deck is built, surround it with a border of flowers or shrubs; this will help soften the transition between the deck and the lawn. Easier still—put pots and planters full of flowers onto the deck itself to add some color.

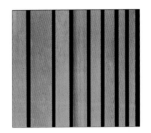

Decking materials are available to suit any budget or design style. Three popular options are pressure-treated wood (top left), redwood (above), and composite (left), such as plastic or wood/plastic blends. Consider cost and maintenance requirements before you buy.

Decks that are 1' or higher off the ground require handrails. Building codes stipulate that the space between the balusters be no greater than 4".

CHECKLIST

✔Save money and use durable pressure-treated lumber for the supports and floor of the deck, and cedar or redwood for rails and trim.

✔Clean mildewed or grungy wood decks with a deck cleaner/brightener. It comes in bleach and nonbleach formulas. Once dry, reseal.

✔Deck kits give you what you pay for—a mass-produced product that may or may not fit your site. It's worth spending a few more dollars to get a custom-designed deck.

TROUBLE

• Deck boards rotting too quickly? Keep the deck free of debris, such as dirt and leaves, that can collect water, resulting in wood rot. Sweep regularly.

• Replacement boards sticking out like a sore thumb? Add years of weathering in minutes by applying a solution of one part baking soda to five parts water. Let stand overnight, then rinse.

• Too windy on the deck? Put up a trellis (see page 148) and plant with vines to help block the wind.

DECK RESOURCES

California Redwood
Association 415-381-0662

Crane Plastics 800-307-7780

DEC-K-ING 800-804-6288

Hickson
Corporation 770-801-6600

Sturdy Structures . . . 630-739-6899

The Thompson's
Company 800-367-6297

POOLS

Adding a swimming pool makes a big splash on the backyard scene. But before you jump into the idea of building one, be certain your site has three things: space for it; access for the excavating equipment; and good exposure to mid-day sun to warm the water after chillier nights and to help keep the water clean of algae.

An aboveground vinyl pool is the least-expensive and fastest to install. A preformed fiberglass pool also saves money and can be installed quickly. Much more expensive are in-ground pools, whether a standard rectangular or a fancy custom shape. Most in-ground pools are made of gunite, a cement mixture applied under high pressure. Others are lined with vinyl.

For custom touches, like many levels and waterfalls, hire an architect, landscape designer, or landscape architect. Ask about special features, such as cantilevered decking and lights for nighttime entertaining.

A good surface area around the pool is vital to safety. Go with wood decking or rough-surfaced tile or concrete to prevent slipping. Most building codes require pools to be fenced.

POOL SAFETY

CHECKLIST ✔If both children and adults will be in the pool, plan a shallow area for toddlers and deeper water for swimmers.

✔Check the manufacturer's specifications before installing a diving board or water slide to make sure your pool is large and deep enough for safe use.

✔Install a fence with a self-latching gate around the pool.

✔Keep life preservers in easy-to-reach locations.

✔Be sure an adult is present when children are in the pool area. Or consider a pool alarm that sounds if there is any agitation in the water.

✔Test pool water every week and replace testing kit each year to ensure that chemicals are fresh.

Aboveground pools are the least-expensive pools to buy and install.

SHORTCUTS •Buy a pool cover to keep water free of debris when not in use in the off seasons.

•Plan on some kind of pool house for storage of pool pump and equipment. If there's room, add on a simple structure to allow for changing.

•Hidden problems, such as underground springs or rocks that can't be moved, can add significantly to the cost of constructing in-ground pools. Ask how these will be handled before you sign a contract.

•Unless you have two hours every weekend to spend on cleaning your pool, hire a pool-maintenance service to get the job done.

POOL SOURCES

Connor's
Pool & Spa 210-520-5095

E.G. Danner
Mfg. Inc. 516-234-5261

Endless Pools, Inc. . . 800-732-8660

Flotec 800-365-6832

Home & Leisure
Center 805-833-6399

Sentinel
Pool & Spa 650-965-4728

Most home insurers and local zoning codes require that in-ground pools be fenced. If privacy is important, consider a solid fence instead of an open wrought-iron fence like this one (see page 44).

KIDS' PLAY AREAS

Keep the ground under the play set as soft as possible. Consider sand, wood chips, or grass to help cushion spills.

Grown-ups, get ready to have some fun. There's more to play sets these days than a metal swing set and sandbox. You can buy ready-made kits that have everything from teeter-totters to pirate-ship lookouts.

Plan your play area with the whole family. Make sure it is away from the garden and your favorite plants but easily accessible to the house and within view from the house. Mark off the play area with string or a hose. A low border of timbers can define the space and double as a bench.

A play area gets a lot of wear, so consider a low-maintenance surface, such as thick layers of sand, smooth pea gravel, or fine bark, to soften falls. Then add equipment, a sandbox or playhouse, and thorn-free shrubs.

You can buy ready-made equipment locally or special-order modular systems. The kits fit together fast in all kinds of combinations, from a play tower and slide to a range of climbing devices with bridges and sitting corners. Some offer add-on units to use as your kids get older. A play system with a variety of equipment is hard to outgrow.

CHECKLIST PLAY AREA SMART
✔Ask your older kids what they would like so you create a site they'll use. Some would rather have a play-house; others like swings and chinning bars. Toddlers like low-angled slides and climbing nets for confidence-building fun.

✔For serious exercise and acrobatics, select equipment with bars, rings, and ladders. Climbing and jumping activities call for multi-level units.

✔Look for rounded, smooth edges and corners, safe angles on climbing equipment, and stability of freestanding designs. Ask about guarantees against splintering and cracking.

✔Add a different element by planting a kid-safe garden next to the play area (see page 138). Sunflowers and other bright blooms are always popular; fragrant herbs are fun to touch and smell.

✔Plan on adding new features as your kids grow up, or start with play systems planned for multi-age use.

PLAY-SET SOURCES

Briar Hill 814-744-9913
Creative Playthings Ltd. 800-735-5460
Handy Home Products 800-221-1849
Oakline Swing Co., Inc. 334-875-1311
Vintage Wood Products 707-585-1717

A very simple sandbox, complete with corner seats, is often the first step in building a children's play area. When not in use, cover with a matching-size piece of plywood to keep out animals.

A plastic play set is a great choice for younger kids since it is free of sharp edges and splinters. Bonus for parents: it is maintenance-free.

SHEDS

Sheds can become an attractive feature in your yard. This shed has been covered with a trellis to hold a climbing Carolina yellow jessamine.

No room in the garage for the car? Then an outbuilding, as it is called, is a must, whether it be a tool-shed, a garden center, or a place to stow all the camping gear.

First, consider location and purpose. Siting a shed sensibly will mean less going back and forth carrying equipment. Put a garden shed near the flowers; attach a simple lean-to to the garage for car tools. And yes, you'll need a building permit. Second, estimate how much storage space you need now, then add 30 to 50 percent more so you don't out-grow it too quickly.

Construction kits are one way to solve the problem. They are a fast, economical, and easy way to build a simple shed. Wooden shed kits are most common. Or get a prefabricated metal or plastic shed if you're in a hurry. Paint it to match your house so that the shed fits into the scheme of things.

Ideally, your shed should do more than just fit in. It should complement your house. To achieve this, you may need to have yours custom-built. You'll probably need a window or two for light. If wall storage is more important than windows, put a skylight in the roof and some decorative trim on an exterior side wall. Consider adding an ornamental feature, such as a cupola, peaked roof, or climbing vine.

PLANNING AND BUILDING

✔ Permanent buildings need solid foundations —and permits. For codes and specifications for the size structure you want, check with your local building department.

✔ Make sure doors lock securely to prevent theft and mishaps with stored chemicals.

✔ Wire your shed for electricity and pipe in running water if you'll use it as a workshop. Add a heating system for year-round use.

TROUBLE • Planning to store liquids and chemicals? Provide good ventilation to keep chemicals safely. Fill containers partway with liquids to leave space for them to expand when freezing.

• Metal shed showing its age? Inexpensive metal sheds offer short-term storage, but some are flimsy, damage easily, and become hard to open and close. Buy good quality to last.

SHED SOURCES

Arrow Group. 800-851-1085

Handy Home Products. 800-221-1849

Lee Valley Tools Ltd. 800-871-8158

Vixen Hill 800-423-2766

GREENHOUSE SOURCES

Elite Greenhouses 800-514-4441

Sunglo Greenhouses. 800-647-0606

Shed doors need to be wide enough to accommodate equipment and allow for trash barrels to move in and out.

GLORIOUS GREENHOUSES

Greenhouses are great additions to the backyard or side of the house. It can double as a potting shed, solarium, and garden room. A true greenhouse provides the moist, warm conditions that plants like. You'll want a ventilation system and lighting to handle excess moisture, and heating for the winter months. A combination greenhouse and sunroom stays drier and can even have a solid roof, as long as there is good eastern, southern, and western exposure.

YARD SAFETY

Low-voltage lighting around walkways and driveways is an energy-efficient way to light your yard at night. Flood lights on the house discourage intruders.

Get a hose holder so you won't trip over the hose.

 CHECKLIST AROUND THE HOUSE

✔ Outdoor lighting: Install floodlights with a motion sensor under the eaves of your house and garage so lights will go on when you or visitors arrive after dark. Motion sensors will also help deter unwanted trespassers—whether two- or four-legged. Install low-voltage lights for smaller areas along pathways and sidewalks.

✔ House key: Hide an extra key to the garage or house in a fake rock key holder. Hide the rock in a flower bed or under a shrub near the front door.

✔ Easy-to-see steps: Put in low-voltage lights or small red reflector lights, or paint a stripe on the edge.

✔ Nonskid steps: Roughen up smooth step surfaces by adding stick-on nonskid strips. For a long flight of steps, put up a handrail.

✔ Trim foundation plantings: Overgrown shrubs and trees can hide an intruder.

✔ Maintain deck and deck railings: replace deteriorated deck boards. Check deck railings; replace or reinforce if loose.

✔ Fire extinguishers: Keep them where you might need them—by the barbecue, in the workshop. (If you live in a rural area and have a pool or a pond, consider investing in a heavy-duty fire hose and generator so that you can put out fires with your own water supply.)

✔ Store flammables safely: Keep your paints, fuels, barbecue starter fluid, and other flammable materials locked up in a well-ventilated storage spot. Keep pest- and weed-control products separate from fertilizers and seeds to avoid any contamination or chemical reactions. Note: Pesticides and herbicides are considered hazardous waste and must be disposed of properly.

✔ Safety reflectors: Attach stick-on reflectors to the mailbox post and to trees near the driveway; install reflector stakes near a drainage ditch and near large boulders. They help you find your way at night and keep cars from damaging your landscape.

✔ Mirrors on driveway: Mount mirrors on the corner of the garage, a fence post, telephone pole, or wherever they will help you get a clear view of the yard as you back out.

✔ De-icer for sidewalks and stoops: Have rock salt or calcium chloride on hand before winter arrives. Keep a large enough supply in the house for a safe exit in case of a surprise storm. Cat litter or small gravel will also work in a pinch to provide good traction over ice.

AROUND THE YARD

CHECKLIST

✔ Inspect trellises and arbors: Heavy vines accumulate dense growth and can weaken their supporting structures. A heavy wind or decaying wood can send them crashing down.

✔ Pruning saw: Have one on hand to remove small dead or weak tree branches at their base before a windstorm blows them down. Store out of reach of children.

✔ Fill large holes with dirt or gravel. Seal off abandoned wells or shafts.

✔ Hose reel: No one will trip over hoses if you roll them up on a reel. Hoses will last longer when you hang them out of the sun.

✔ Check for ticks: Where deer are plentiful, look for pinhead-size ticks that may carry Lyme disease. Wear tight, light-colored clothing if you are going to be outside long; they'll be easier to spot. Check pets, too; they can easily carry deer ticks into the house on their fur or skin.

✔ Safety goggles: Wear them when you operate a chain saw, wood chipper, or weed trimmer (see page 52).

✔ Fence water ponds or pools: Most home insurers require fences with secure gates around bodies of water. Also, get a pool alarm that sounds if someone falls into your pool.

✔ Identify any toxic plants in your yard and remove them safely.

✔ Mole and gopher traps: Catch burrowing critters that leave dangerous holes in the lawn. Traps are more reliable and safer around pets than poison baits.

✔ Hornet traps: Set out traps for hornets and yellow jackets if they are threatening children playing outside.

✔ Wear ear protectors: Protect ears from noise damage when using excessively loud chains saws, shredders, lawn mowers, and blowers. Headsets offer more protection than individual earplugs.

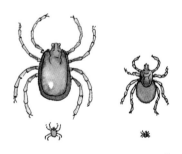

A pool alarm sounds when water is disturbed.

Ticks are unpleasant, blood-sucking pests. Dog ticks are shown enlarged and actual size (left). Deer ticks, which can carry Lyme disease, are shown enlarged and actual size (right). If you are bitten by a deer tick, call your doctor.

Plastic, locking storage cabinet for tools and chemicals.

SAFETY RESOURCES

The Brinkmann
Corporation 800-527-0717

D & D
Technologies, Inc. . . 800-716-0888

First Alert, Inc. 800-392-1395

Intermatic Malibu . . 815-675-2321

Lambo Products, Inc.415-965-4728

National Safety
Council 800-621-7619

INDEX

SUBJECT

A
Aerators, 55
Air circulation, 31, 39, 121
Aluminum sulfate, adding to soil, 34
Animal repellent, 137
Annuals
  begonias, 111
  buying, 110
  defined, 110
  guide, 108-109
  hardiness, 110, 111
  how to plant, 108-109
  impatiens, 111
  marigolds, 112
  pansies, 112
  planting time for, 110
  salvias, 113
  starting from seeds or seedlings, 112
  wilted, 112
  zinnias, 113
Antidesiccant sprays, 31, 87
Aphids, 101, 133
Arbors, 142-143, 148-149
Asphalt driveways, 21
Attracting
  birds, 15, 105, 139
  butterflies, 139
Azaleas, 98-99

B
Backyards
  defined, 10
  defining specialty areas, 16
  how to divide side yard from, 14
  providing privacy, 16
Balled and burlapped, 95, 99, 101
Bare-root plants, 101
Basements, water in, 37
Beetles, 39
Birds, how to attract, 15, 105, 139
Blackspot, 133
Building permits, 17, 152
Bulbs
  crocuses, 115
  daffodils, 115
  defined, 114
  didn't come up, reasons for, 117
  forcing, 116
  guide, 108-109
  how to buy and plant, 108-109, 114

hyacinths, 116
jonquils, 116
lilies, 117
tulips, 117
Bulb planter, 108
Burlap, use of, 29, 95, 129
Butterflies, attracting, 139

C
Catch basins, 36
Caterpillars, 131
Children's play areas, 17
  guide, 142-143
  planning tips, 156-157
Children's gardens
  flowers that attract wildlife to, 139
  guide, 126-127
  helpful hints, 138, 139
Christmas trees, planting of, 75
Clay soil, 32
Climate
  elements, 30-31
  guide, 26-27
  winterizing plants, tips for, 29
  zones, 28-29
Cold spots, plantings for, 26
Compost, 32
  bins, 33
  materials for, 32-33
Concrete
  driveways, 21
  pavers, precast, 21
  patios, 150-151
Container gardens
  in backyards, 16
  guide, 126-127
  how to fill containers, 134
  location for, 135
  problems with, 135
  in side yards, 15
  types of containers, 134, 135
Corms, 114

D
Deadheading, 105, 118, 133
Decks, 16, 152-153
  building permits, 152
  cleaning, 153
  guide, 142-143
  how to weather boards, 153
  planning tips, 152
  sealants and stains, 152
  windbreaks for, 153

Deer, 137
Detail drawings, 8
Discolored leaves, meaning of, 35
Diseases, home remedies, 39
Drainage
  basements, problems in, 37
  ditches/trenches, 36, 37
  grading and, 36, 37
  guide, 26-27
  patio, 151
  pipes, 36
  problems, how to fix, 36, 37
  slope and, 37
  testing soil, 33, 35
  tips before making repairs, 37
Driveways
  circular, 20
  determining width of, 20, 21
  materials for, pros and cons of, 21
  mirrors on, 161
  plantings along, 20
  snowplowing, 21
  turnarounds, 20, 21
  walkways to, 20
Dry wells, 36

E
Ear protectors, 161
Earthworms, 32
Easements, 8
Edgers, 55
Edging, for walkways, 19
Elements
  sunlight, 30, 31
  wind, 30, 31
Espalier, 15
Evergreens
  browning of lower branches, 73
  dropping of needles/leaves, 73
  as hedges, 87
  location for, 72
  selection and planting of, 73
  shrubs as foundation plants, 12
  trees, 72-73
  winter protection for, 31

F
Fencing
  camouflaging, 145
  checklist, 145
  evergreens as, 72
  guide, 142-143
  hedges as, 84-89

ordinances, 144
  around pools, 154, 155
  for privacy, 16, 144
  styles of, 144, 144
  as a windbreak, 30, 31
Feng Shui, 23
Fertilizer/fertilizing
  bags, how to read, 35
  container plants, 135
  evergreens, 73
  guide, 26-27
  hedges, 85
  lawns, 48
  liquid, 35
  roses, 133
  shrub roses, 103
  synthetic versus organic, 35
  when to apply, 35
Firewood, storage of, 15
Flower beds
  colors in, 108
  location of, 17, 19
Flowering trees
  nonflowering, 75
  selection and planting of, 74-75
Flowering vines, 104-105
Forcing bulbs, 116
Formal landscape designs
  house styles for, 10
  walkway shape and materials for, 18
Formal hedges, 84
Formal yards
  defined, 10
  maintenance of, 11
Foundation-plant pointers, 12, 13
Foundations
  grading problems around, 37
  how to soften lines, 11, 12
  raised planters to conceal, 13
Freestanding walls, 146
Front doors, more than one, 13
Front yards
  checklist, 13
  defined, 10
  foundation plants, 12, 13
  how to break up large, 13
  walkways, 12
Frost pockets, 29
Fruit/nut trees
  problems with, 79
  selection and care of, 78-79

Fungi, 31
Fungicidal soap, 39
Fungicides, 38, 121, 133, 160

G

Georgian houses, 10
Grading soil, 36, 44
Grass
  choices, for lawns, 45, 51
  ornamental, 12, 64-65
  removing, from lawns, 33, 61
Gravel driveways, 21
Greek Revival houses, 10
Greenhouses, 159
Ground covers, 13
  buying and planting, 58-59, 61
  guide, 58-59
  ornamental grasses, 64-65
  for shady areas, 62-63
  for sunny areas, 60-61

H

Hardiness
  annuals and, 110, 111
  defined, 110
  zones, 28, 29
Hardscape, 13, 22, 141
Hedges
  boundary, 86-87
  camouflage, 88-89
  evergreen, 87, 91
  formal versus informal, 84
  guide, 82-83
  privacy, 16, 17, 84-85
  problems with, 85, 87, 89, 91
  pruning, 82-83, 84, 85, 86, 89
  selection and planting of, 82-83, 85, 87, 89, 91
  shrub roses as, 102
  thorny, 90-91
  as windbreaks, 30, 86
Hedge shears, 82
Herb garden. See Kitchen gardens
Herbicidal soaps, 38
Herbicides, 38, 54
Home remedies, 39
Hornet/yellow jacket traps, 161
Horticultural oil, 38
House styles
  walkways based on, 18
  yard design based on, 10-11

I

Informal landscape designs
  house styles for, 10-11
  walkway shape and materials for, 18
Informal hedges, 84
  hydrangeas as, 96
Informal yards, defined, 10
Insecticidal soaps, 38
Insecticides, 38, 54, 131
Insects. See Pests
Irrigation systems, 51
  illustrated, 42-43

K

Kitchen gardens, 15
  guide, 126-127
  location for, 136, 137
  pests and, 137

L

Ladybugs, 39
Landscape architects, 8, 11, 22
Landscape blueprint, 8-9
Landscape contractors, 8, 22
Landscape design
  backyards, 16-17
  driveways, 20-21
  front yards, 12-13
  guide, 8-9
  planning, 10-11
  professionals, 22-23
  side yards, 14-15
  walkways, 18-19
Landscape designers, 8, 11, 22
Lawn equipment
  hand versus power, 55
  irrigation systems, 51
  mowers/trimmers, 52-53
Lawn(s)
  fertilizing, 48
  guide, 42-43
  mowing, 48-49
  overseeding existing, 46-47
  patches of brown/dead grass, 49, 51
  preparing for new, 44-45
  puddles, 37
  seeding versus laying down sod, 44
  services, 23, 53
  watering, 45, 50-51
Leaf spot, 39
Leggy plants, 30, 110
Licensing of professionals, 22
Lighting, 160

Lime, adding to soil, 34, 35
Loamy soil, 32

M

Master plan, 8-9
Midges, 103
Mildew, 31
Milorganite, 137
Modern house designs, 11
Mole/gopher traps, 161
Mowers
  illustrated by type, 42-43
  problems with, 53
  selection tips, 53
  types of, 52
Mowing, 48-49
Mulch
  adding, 32
  around evergreens, 73
  coco hulls, 58
  hard versus soft, 32
  for insulating plants, 29
  types of, 73, 85, 87
  wood bark or chips, 61, 89
  weed control and, 39
Mulching lawn mowers, 52

N

Nitrogen, 35
Noise, how to block out, 17
Nutrients, essential soil, 34-35
Nut trees, 78-79

O

Organic matter, 32, 47, 105

P

Patios, 16
  drainage problems, 151
  guide, 142-143
  maintaining, 151
  paving materials and patterns for, 150
  preventing weeds, 151
  slippery, 151
  tips for building, 150
Pavers
  concrete precast, 21
  interlocking, 18, 19
Peat moss, 32, 61
Perennials
  asters, 119
  astilbes, 119
  chrysanthemums, 120
  daisies, 120
  daylilies, 121

dividing, 121,
dividing, illustrated, 108
forget-me-nots, 121
as foundation plants, 12
geraniums, 122
guide, 108-109
irises, 122
peonies, 123
phlox, 123
planting, 108-109, 118
problems with, 121
Pergolas, 142-143, 148-149
Pesticides, 38, 121, 133, 160
Pests
  See also under type of
  controlling, 38-39, 54, 137
  guide to, 26-27
  on hedges, 89
  home remedies, 39
  in kitchen gardens, 137
  in rock gardens, 151
  on roses, 133
  on shrub roses, 103
  on viburnums, 101
pH
  how to raise or lower, 34
  testing, 34, 35
Phosphorous, 35
Planning landscape, 10-11
Planting guide
  annuals, 108-109
  bulbs, 108-109
  ground covers, 58-59
  hedges, 82-83
  perennials, 108-109
  shrubs, 94-95
  trees, 68-69
Playsets, 156-157
Pools, 154-155
  alarms, 161
  fencing around, 154, 155
  guide, 142-143
  maintenance, 155
  planning tips, 154
  safety tips, 155
Potassium, 35
Powdery mildew, 39, 97, 121, 133
Professionals
  bids from, 23
  Feng Shui, 23
  hiring tips, 23

insurance coverage, 23
lawn services, 23
licensing of, 22
types of, 23
Pruning
  hedges, 84, 85, 86, 89
  hydrangeas, 97
  rhododendrons/azaleas, 99
  saw, 161
  trees, 68-69

R

Rabbits, 137
Rakes, 55
Ramps, 19
Ranch-style houses, 11
Retaining walls, 146, 147
Rhizomes, 114
Rock gardens, 33
  guide, 126-127
  how to create and maintain, 131
  plants for, 130
  problems with, 131
Roof lines, how to soften, 11
Rose gardens
  guide, 126-127
  planting and care of, 133
  problems with, 133
  types for, 132, 133
Roses, shrub, 102-103
Rototiller, use of, 33, 46
Rust fungi, 39, 133

S

Safety
  goggles, 161
  around the house, 160
  pool, 155
  yard, 160-161
Salt-tolerant shrubs, 31, 102
Sandy soil, 32
Scale, 101
Shade and partial shade
  defined, 30
  grass for, 47
  ground covers for, 62-63
  plants for, 31
Shade trees, 70-71
Sheds
  guide, 142-143
  planning and building, 158-159
Shrubs
  flowering vines, 104-105

guide, 94-95
hydrangeas, 96-97
mulching around, 94-95
problems with, 97, 101, 103, 105
pruning, 94-95, 97, 99
rhododendrons/azaleas, 98-99
roses, 102-103
salt-tolerant shrubs, 31, 102
selection and planting of, 94-95, 97, 99,
  101, 103, 105
viburnums, 100-101
Side yards
  defined, 10
  how to divide from backyard, 14
  how to enlarge, 14
  tips for, 15
  walkways for, 19
Site inventory, 8
Silt soil, 32
Slopes, steep, 13, 17
Slugs/snails, 38, 39, 63, 131
Snow
  as an insulator, 29
  plowing driveways, 21
  protecting evergreens from, 29
Soil
  acidic versus alkaline, 34
  amendments, 34
  compacted, test for, 45
  conditioners, adding, 32, 33
  drainage, testing for, 33
  essential nutrients, 34-35
  grading, 36, 44
  guide, 26-27
  pH, 34-35
  rocky or soggy, 33
  testing, 34, 35
  texture, determining, 32, 33, 50
  tips for improving, 33
Spider mites, 89, 101
Spreaders, 55
Sprinklers, 51
Staking, 68, 73, 121
Stepping stones, preformed, 19
Stone walls
  battered, 146
  checklist, 147
  colors of stone, 146
  dry-stacked versus mortared, 146
  freestanding, 146-147
  guide, 142-143

problems with, 147
to protect plants, 29
retaining, 146-147
Sulfur, adding to soil, 34
Sunlight patterns
  full sun, 30
  partial sun/shade, 30
  shade, 30
Sunny areas, ground covers for, 60-61

T

Thatch buildup, 49
Thatch rake, 55
Thrips, 101, 103
Ticks, 161
Tool sheds, 14, 15
Trees
  buying, 71
  Christmas, 73
  distance from houses, 13
  dwarf, 13, 76, 78
  evergreens, 72-73
  flowering, 74-75
  fruit/nut, 78-79
  ground covers under, 65
  guide, 68-69
  planting, 68-69
  problems with, 71, 73, 75, 77, 79
  professionals, 23
  pruning, 68-69
  shade, 70-71
  specialty, 76-77
Trellises, 142-143, 148-149, 153
Trimmers, 52-53
Tuber-corms, 114
Tubers, 114

U

Utilities
  drainage work and locating, 37
  hiding, 17
  planning and locating, 11

V

Vegetable garden. See Kitchen gardens
Vines
  flowering, 104-105
  planting, 94-95

W

Walkways
  edging for, 19
  house styles and design of, 18
  how to soften lines, 12, 18
  lighting for, 160

materials for, leading to driveways, 20
materials for high-traffic areas, 18
materials for steps, 19
ramps, 19
for side yards, 19
use of, 10
width of front, 12
width of main, 18
width of secondary, 18
Warm spots, plantings for, 26
Water gardens
  fish in, 128, 129
  guide, 126-127
  how to create, 128-129
  plants for, 128
  problems with, 129
  where to locate, 26
Watering
  depth, 42, 50-51, 133
  flowers, 108
  hedges, 85, 87
  ground covers, 58
  lawns, 45, 50-51
  trees, 68, 73
Weeders, 55
Weeds, 55
  controlling, 38-39, 54, 151
  guide to, 26-27
  home remedies, 39
Winds
  antidesiccant sprays as protection, 31, 87
  how to diminish effects of, 30
Windbreaks, 30, 31
  for decks, 153
  evergreens as, 72
  fencing as, 144
  hedges as, 26-27, 86
Winter dieback, 103
Winterizing plants, tips for, 29
Woodchucks, 137

Y

Yellow jacket traps, 161

PLANT NAMES

Each plant has a unique scientific name (in Latin) and one or more common names. Since common names are applied to more than one plant species, you can avoid confusion by using scientific names. Full scientific names consist of a plant's genus followed by its species, both of which are printed in italics, and, if needed, by a variety name or a cultivar name in single quotes. Here we list the common name first, then its Latin name.

A

African daisy—*Gerbera*, 111
Ajuga—*Ajuga*, 60
American arborvitae—*Thuja occidentalis*, 85, 87
American hornbeam—*Carpinus caroliniana*, 70-71
American sweetgum—*Liquidambar styraciflua*, 70-71
Apple—*Malus*, 78-79
  crab apple, 15, 74
  'Donald Wyman' crabapple, 74-75
Aster—*Aster*, 119, 123
  China aster, 111
  Michaelmas daisy, 119
Astilbe—*Astilbe*, 119, 123
Azalea—*Rhododendron*, 98-99
  Glenn Dale hybrids, 98-99
  Kurume hybrids, 98-99
  Robin Hill hybrids, 98-99

B

Basil—*Ocimum*, 136-137
Basket-of-gold—*Aurinia*, 130-131
Bee balm—*Monarda*, 138-139
Begonia—*Begonia*, 113
  wax begonia, 111
Bermuda grass—*Cynodon dactylon*, 45, 49, 51
Blue grama—*Bouteloua gracilis*, 51
Bougainvillea—*Bougainvillea*, 104-105
Boxwood—*Buxus*, 85, 89
Buffalo grass—*Buchlöe dactyloides*, 51
Butterfly bush—*Buddleia davidii*, 138-139

C

California privet—*Ligustrum ovalifolium*, 86-87
Candytuft—*Iberis sempervirens*, 130-131
Celosia—*Celosia*, 111
Cherry,—*Prunus* 78-79

cherry laurel, 86-87
  flowering cherry, 74-75
Chrysanthemum—*Chrysanthemum* 120, 123, 135
  Daisy, 120, 123
Citrus—*Citrus*, 79
Clematis—*Clematis*, 104-105
Cornelian cherry—*Cornus mas*, 84-85
Cornflower—*Centaurea cyanus*, 111
Cosmos—*Cosmos*, 111
Cotoneaster—*Cotoneaster*, 15
Creeping thyme—*Thymus*, 18-19, 60
Creeping veronica—*Veronica prostrata*, 130-131
Crocus—*Crocus*, 63, 115, 117
Cucumber—*Cucumis sativus*, 137
Cypress—*Cupressus*
  Italian cypress, 89
  Leyland cypress, 88-89

D

Daffodil—*Narcissus*, 63, 115, 117
Daisy. See Chrysanthemum
Dalmatian bellflower—*Campanula portenschlagiana*, 18-19
Daylily—*Hemerocallis*, 121, 123
Dogwood—*Cornus*, 15
  Cornelian cherry, 84-85
  flowering dogwood, 74-75

E

Eastern red cedar—*Juniperus virginiana*, 88-89. *See also* Juniper
Eel grass—*Vallisneria americana*, 128-129
Elm—*Ulmus*, 71
Euonymus—*Euonymus*, 60-61
  winged euonymus, 15

F

Fescue grass—*Festuca*, 71
  blue fescue, 64-65
  chewings fescue, 51
  fine fescue, 45, 47, 49
  hard fescue, 51
  red fescue, 51
Fir—*Abies*, 72-73, 76
Fire thorn—*Pyracantha*, 90-91
Flowering tobacco—*Nicotiana alata*, 111
Forget-me-not—*Myosotis*, 121, 123
Fountain grass—*Pennisetum alopecuroides*, 64-65
Fraser photinia—*Photinia* x *fraseri*, 88-89

G

Geranium—*Geranium*, 122-123, 135
Giant feather grass—*Stipa gigantea*, 64-65
Grape hyacinth—*Muscari*, 115
Grapefruit—*Citrus* × *paradisi*, 78
Grecian windflower—*Anemone*, 115

H

Hawthorn—*Crataegus*
  Washington hawthorn, 90-91
  'Winter King' hawthorn, 76-77
Heliotrope—*Heliotropium*, 111
Hemlock—*Tsuga*, 85, 89
  Canadian hemlock, 84, 89
  weeping hemlock, 15
Holly—*Ilex*, 72-73
  American holly, 86-87
  Japanese holly, 89
  Winterberry, 15
Honeylocust—*Gleditsia*
  'Sunburst', 77
  thornless honeylocust, 70-71
Honeysuckle—*Lonicera sempervirens*, 104-105
Hosta—*Hosta*, 62-63
Hyacinth—*Hyacinthus*, 116-117
Hydrangeas—*Hydrangea*, 87, 96-97

I

Ice plant—*Carpobrotus, Cephalophyllum, Deloserma, Drosanthemum, Lampranthus, Malephora*, 60
Impatiens—*Impatiens*, 111, 113
Iris—*Iris*, 122-123
Ivy—*Hedera*, 62-63

J

Japanese barberry—*Berberis thunbergii*, 90-91
Japanese zelkova—*Zelkova serrata*, 70-71
Jasmine—*Jasminum officinale*, 104-105
Joe-Pye weed—*Eupatorium*, 138-139
Jonquil—*Narcissus*, 116-117
Juniper—*Juniperus*, 15, 60-61, 88
  Chinese juniper, 89
  Eastern red cedar, 88-89
Jupiter's beard—*Centranthus*, 138-139

K

Kangaroo thorn—*Acacia armata*, 90-91
Kentucky bluegrass—*Poa pratensis*, 45, 49

L

Larkspur—*Consolida*, 111
Leaf lettuce—*Lactuca sativa*, 136-137
Lemon—*Citrus limon*, 78

Lily—*Lilium*, 117
Lily-of-the-valley—*Convallaria*, 62-63
Lime—*Citrus aurantiifolia*, 78
Lotus—*Nelumbo*, 128-129

M

Maiden grass—*Miscanthus sinensis* 'Gracillimus', 64-65
Maple—*Acer*
  Japanese maple, 76-77
  paperbark maple, 76-77
  red maple, 71
  sugar maple, 70-71
Marigold—*Tagetes*, 112-113, 135
Mountain ash—*Sorbus*, 15

N

Nasturtium—*Tropaeolum*, 111

O

Orange—*Citrus sinensis*, 78
Oregano—*Origanum vulgare*, 136-137

P

Pachysandra—*Pachysandra*, 62-63
Pansy—*Viola*, 112-113, 135
Parsley—*Petroselinum*, 136-137
Peach—*Prunus persica*, 78-79
Pecan—*Carya illinoinensis*, 78-79
Peony—*Paeonia*, 123
Periwinkle—*Vinca*, 62-63
Petunia—*Petunia*, 111, 135
Phlox—*Phlox*, 123
  moss phlox, 18-19
Pine—*Pinus* 72-73, 76
  weeping pine, 77
Pittosporum—*Pittosporum tobira*, 85
Poison ivy—*Toxicodendron radicans*, 63
Poplar—*Populus*, 71
Poppy—*Papaver*, 111
Portulaca—*Portulaca*, 111
Purple coneflower—*Echinacea purpurea*, 138-139
Purple rock cress—*Aubrieta deltoidea*, 130-131

Q

Quaking grass, perennial—*Briza media*, 65

R

Red horse chestnut—*Aesculus* × *carnea*, 74-75
Redbud—*Cercis canadensis*, 74-75
Rhododendron—*Rhododendron*, 98-99
  Catawba, 98-99
  Fortunei hybrids, 98-99

Rosebay, 98-99
Ribbon grass–*Phalaris arundinacea* var.
 picta, 64, 65
Rose–*Rosa*, 102-103, 132-133
 'Cécile Brunner', 132-133
 English rose hybrids, 102-103
 Father Hugo's rose, 102-103
 'Margaret Merril', 132-133
 Meidiland™, 102-103
 'Morden Centennial', 132-133
 musk hybrid, 102, 103
 rugosa rose, 90, 91, 102-103
 'Sunsprite', 132-133
 'William Baffin', 132-133
Ryegrass, perennial–*Lolium perenne*, 45

S
Salvia–*Salvia*, 113
Sedum–*Sedum*, 60
Serviceberry–*Amelanchier*, 15
Siberian squill–*Scilla siberica*, 115
Silver mound artemesia–*Artemesia schmid-*
 tiana 'Silver Mound', 130-131
Snapdragon–*Antirrhinum*, 111
Snowdrop–*Galanthus*, 63, 115
Southern live oak–*Quercus virginiana*, 70-71
Southern magnolia–*Magnolia grandiflora*,
 74-75
Spanish bluebell–*Endymion hispanicus*, 115
Spruce–*Picea*, 72-73, 76
 dwarf Alberta spruce, 15
St. Augustine grass–*Stenotaphrum secunda-*
 tum, 45, 47, 49
Sugar maple–*Acer saccharum*, 67
Sunflower–*Helianthus*, 139, 157
Sweet alyssum–*Lobularia*, 18-19
Sweet woodruff–*Galium odoratum*, 62-63

T
Tomato–*Lycopersicum*, 137, 139
Trumpet creeper–*Campsis radicans*, 104-
 105, 139
Tulip–*Tulipa*, 117

V
Viburnum–*Viburnum*, 15, 100-101
 American cranberry, 84-85, 100
 black haw, 86-87
 David, 100
 doublefile, 100
 Korean spice, 100-101
 Laurustinus, 100

W
Wall rock cress–*Arabis caucasica*, 130-131
Walnut–*Juglans*, 78-79
Water lettuce–*Pistia stratiotes*, 128-129
Water lily–*Nymphaea* 128-129
Water milfoil–*Myriophyllum pinnatum*, 128-
 129
Willow–*Salix*, 71
Winterberry–*Ilex*, 15
Wisteria–*Wisteria*, 104-105, 149

Y
Yaupon–*Ilex vomitoria*, 72-73
Yellow flag–*Iris pseudacoris*, 128-129
Yew–*Taxus*, 85, 87, 89

Z
Zinnia–*Zinnia*, 113
Zoysia grass–*Zoysia matrella*, 45, 49

RESOURCES

A
A & L Eastern Agricultural Labs, Inc., 35
A. M. Andrews Co., 51
Advanced Drainage Systems, Inc., 37
AgrEvo Environmental Health, 39, 54
Aimcor Consumer Products L.L.C., 33
Al's Garden Art, 135
American Boxwood Society, 81
American Feng Shui Institute, 23
American Lawn Mower Co., 53
American Rhododendron Society, 99
American Rose Society, 103
Anderson Design, R.L., 151
Aquapore Moisture Systems, Inc., 4, 139
Arboria Garden Structures, 149
Arrow Group, 159
Associated Landscape Contractors of
 America, 23
Association of Professional Landscape
 Designers, 23

B
Backyard Products, 19, 149
Beaty Fertilizer Co., Inc., 35
Berkeley Forge & Foundry, 151
Black & Decker, 53
Bluestone Perennials, 57
Bonide Products, Inc., 39
Breck's Dutch Bulbs, 117
Briar Hill, 157
Brinkmann Corporation, 161
Brown's Kalmia & Azalea, 99
Bufftech, Inc., 145

C
California Redwood Association, 153
Carroll Gardens, Inc., 57, 97, 101
Connor's Pool & Spa, 155
Crane Plastics, Inc., 153
Creative Playthings, Ltd., 157

D
Daffodil Mart, 117
D & D Technologies Inc., 161
DEC-K-ING, 153
DeGiorgi Seeds & Goods, 137
Dutch Gardens, 117

E
Earthgro, 33, 35
Easy Gardener, 35
Edmund's Roses, 133
EG Danner Mfg. Inc., 155

Elite Greenhouses, 159
Endless Pools, Inc., 155
Enviroedge Products Company, 145

F
Far West Forests, 33
Feng Shui Warehouse, Inc., 23
Ferry-Morse Seed Co., 139
First Alert, Inc., 161
Flotec, 155
Forest Farm, 67, 81

G
Garden Crafters Inc., 135
Gardener's Supply Co., 4, 33, 135
Gardeners Eden, 33, 135
Gardens Alive, 39, 54
Gardner Asphalt Corp., 21
Gibson Homans, 21
Gilbert H. Wild & Son LLC, 123
Gilbertie's Herbs, 137
Great Western Seed, 45
Green Glen Nursery, Inc., 67
Greer Gardens, 99
Gurney's Seed & Nursery Co., 33, 67, 81,
 113, 137

H
Halquist Stone Company, 19, 21, 147
Handy Home Products, 157, 159
Hayes Company, 149
Heritage Rose Foundation, 133
Hickson Corporation, 153
Home & Leisure Center, 155

I
Intermatic Malibu, 161
Island Post Cap, 149

J
Jackson & Perkins, 103, 133
John Deere, 53
Johnny's Selected Seeds, 137
John Scheepers, 117

K
Kinsman Company, Inc., 135
Klehm Nursery, 123
Krukowski Stone Co., Inc., 147, 151

L
L. R. Nelson Corporation, 51
Lambo Products, Inc., 161
Landscape Architecture Foundation, 23
Lawn-Boy, 53
Lee Valley Tools Ltd., 33, 139, 159

Lester's Material Service, Inc., 33, 37
Lilypons Water Gardens, 129
Little Giant Pump Company, 129
Lofts Seed, Inc., 45
Luster Leaf Products, Inc., 35

M

Milaeger's Inc., 57, 105
Milestones Products Company, 19
Miller Nurseries, Inc., 67, 105
Mister Boardwalk, 19
Moultrie Manufacturing Company, 145
Musser Forests Inc., 67, 81, 99

N

NAAN Sprinklers & Irrigation Systems,
   Inc., 51
National Arborist Association, Inc., 23
National Safety Council, 161
Newport Garden Structures, 149

O

Oakline Swing Co., Inc., 157
Oldcastle Homecenter Group, 147, 151
Ortho Books, 39

P

Paradise Water Gardens LTD, 129
Park Seed Company, 4, 113, 137
Paveloc Industries, 19, 21
Peaceful Valley Farm Supply, 54
Peekskill Nurseries, 57
Pennington Seed, Inc., 45, 54
Perry's Water Gardens, 129
Plow & Hearth, 4
Professional Lawn Care Association of
   America, 23

R

Rauch Clay Sales Corp., 147
Ringer Corporation, 54
Rocks, Etc., Inc., 21, 147, 151
Roseraie at Bay Fields, 103, 133
Rowe Pottery Works, 135

S

Safer, Inc., 39
Savage Nursery, 67
Savory's Gardens, Inc., 57
Schreiner's Gardens, 123
Scotts Company, 35, 39, 45, 54
Seasons Irrigation Supply, 51
Sentinel Pool and Spas, 155
Shepherd Hill Farm, 99
Shepherd's Garden Seeds, 139
Sierra Jane's Trading Company, 19

Slocum Water Gardens, 129
Smith & Hawken, 4
Soleno SPD Inc., 37
Spring Hill Nurseries, 4, 57, 81, 97, 103,
   105, 123
Stark Brothers Nurseries, 67
Stokes Seeds, Inc., 4, 137
Sturdy Structures, 153
Submatic Irrigation Systems, 51
Sunglo Greenhouses, 159

T

Thompson and Morgan, 105, 113
Thompsons Company, 145, 153
Toro, 53
Troy-Bilt, 53
Turfgrass Producers International, 45

U

UNI-Group U.S.A., 21
Union Tools, 139

V

Van Bourgondien's, 117
Van Dyck's, 117
Vermont Maple Mulch, 33
Vintage Wood Products, 145, 157
Vixen Hill, 159

W

W. Atlee Burpee Co., 4, 113
Wayside Gardens, 57, 97, 101, 123
White Flower Farm, 4, 57, 97, 101, 103,
   105, 123
Whiting Nursery, 133
Woods End Research Laboratory, Inc., 35

CREDITS

PICTURE

P.5 top Crandall & Crandall; p.5 bottom Design House, Inc.; p.7 Gay Bumgarner; p.11 Jerry Howard/Positive Images; p.12 Gay Bumgarner; p.13 Crandall & Crandall; p.14 Roger Foley; p.15 top Lee Lockwood/Positive Images; p.15 bottom left Karen Bussolini/Positive Images; p.15 Lee Valley Tools Ltd.; p.16 Robert Walch; p.17 Crandall & Crandall; p.18 Jerry Pavia; p.19 top Gay Bumgarner; p.19 bottom Crandall & Crandall; p.20 Crandall & Crandall; p.21 top Gay Bumgarner; p.21 bottom Crandall & Crandall; p.22 Crandall & Crandall; p.23 top Crandall & Crandall; p.23 bottom Candace Cochrane/Positive Images; p.25 Daniel Clark; p.29 top Lee Lockwood/Positive Images; p.29 bottom Margaret Hensel/Positive Images; p.30 Ken Druse; p.31 top left Crandall & Crandall; p.31 top right Patricia Bruno/Positive Images; p.31 bottom Patricia Bruno/Positive Images; p.32 all photos Derek Fell; p.33 Gardener's Supply Company; p.34 Lee Lockwood/Positive Images; p.35 bottom left Kevin Kennefick; top right Jerry Pavia; p.36 Advanced Drainage Systems; p.37 top Jerry Howard/Positive Images; p.37 bottom Crandall & Crandall; p.38 Crandall & Crandall; p.39 top left and right Bill Johnson; p.39 bottom Crandall & Crandall; p.41 Allan Mandell; p.44 Jerry Howard/Positive Images; p.45 J. Paul Moore; p.46 Allan Mandell; p.47 Crandall & Crandall; p.48 Jerry Howard/Positive Images; p.49 Kathlene Persoff; p.50 A.M. Andrews Company; p.51 Crandall & Crandall; p.52 John Deere; p.53 Black & Decker; p.54 Crandall & Crandall; p.55 bottom left Troy Bilt; p.55 bottom left silo. Union Tools; p.55 bottom center and right Lee Valley Tools Ltd.; p.55 center right Crandall & Crandall; p.55 top Clark's Aerators; p.57 Crandall & Crandall; p.60 Dency Kane; p.61 top left Gay Bumgarner; p.61 top right Richard Shiell; p.62 Dency Kane; p.63 top center R. Todd Davis; p.63 top right Clark's Aerators; p.64 Crandall & Crandall; p.65 Roger Foley; p.67 Pam Spaulding/Positive Images; p.70 Richard Shiell; p.71 Derek Fell; p.72 Jerry Pavia; p.73 left Roger Foley; p.73 center Jerry Howard/Positive Images; p.74 Allan Mandell; p.75 Karen Bussolini/Positive Images; p.76 Crandall & Crandall; p.77 top Derek Fell; p.77 bottom Pam Spaulding/Positive Images; p.78 left Jerry Howard/Positive Images; p.78 right Jerry Pavia; p.79 top and bottom Harry Haralambou/Positive Images; p.81 Dency Kane; p.82 Black & Decker; p.84 Crandall & Crandall; p.85 Derek Fell; p.86 Jerry Pavia; p.87 Jerry Pavia; p.88 Kathlene Persoff; p.89 Richard Shiell; p.90 Ken Druse; p.91 Derek Fell; p.93 Richard Shiell; p.96 Dency Kane; p.97 top Ken Druse; p.97 bottom Jerry Pavia; p.98 Roger Foley; p.99 top Jerry Howard/Positive Images; p.99 bottom Paul Rezendes/Positive Images; p.100 Joseph G. Strauch, Jr.; p.101 top Jerry Pavia; p.101 bottom Allan Mandell; p.102 Roger Foley; p.103 top Clark's Aerators; p.103 bottom Michael Dodge/White Flower Farm; p.104 Patricia Bruno/Positive Images; p.105 Margaret Hensel/Positive Images; p.107 Harry Haralambou/Positive Images; p.111 top Thomas Eltzroth; p.111 bottom Jerry Pavia; p.112 top Jack Foley/Positive Images; p.112 bottom Lee Anne White/Positive Images; p.113 left Pam Spaulding/Positive Images; p.113 center Roger Foley; p.115 left Breck's; p.115 Kathlene Persoff; p.116 bottom left Crate & Barrel; p.116 top right Jerry Pavia; p.116 bottom right Joseph G. Strauch, Jr.; p.117 top left Gay Bumgarner; p.117 center Roger Foley; p.119 top left Jerry Pavia; p.119 top right R. Todd Davis; p.120 top and bottom Jerry Howard/Positive Images; p.121 top Jerry Howard/Positive Images; p.121 bottom Thomas Eltzroth; p.122 top Harry Haralambou/Positive Images; p.122 bottom Crandall & Crandall; p.123 left Roger Foley; p.123 right Jerry Pavia; p.125 Crandall & Crandall; p.128 Dency Kane; p.129 top left David Falconer; p.129 top center Lilypons Water Gardens; p.129 bottom center Roger Foley; p.130 Jerry Pavia; p.131 top Allan Mandell; p.131 bottom Crandall & Crandall; p.132 Jerry Pavia; p.133 left and left center Dency Kane; p.133 right and right center Richard Shiell; p.134 Jerry Pavia; p.135 both photos Kinsman Company; p.136 Lee Anne White/Positive Images; p.137 Jerry Howard/Positive Images; p.138 Dency Kane; p.139 top left Pam Spaulding/Positive Images; p.139 top center Lee Lockwood/Positive Images; p.139 top right Jerry Howard/Positive Images; p.139 bottom left Jerry Pavia; p.139 bottom center Gay Bumgarner; p.139 bottom right Harry Haralambou/Positive Images; p.141 Roger Foley; p.144 Tom Rider/California Redwood Association; p.145 top Jerry Pavia; p.145 bottom Gay Bumgarner; p.146 ©The Reader's Digest Association, Inc.; p.147 J. Paul Moore; p.148 Jerry Pavia; p.149 left Crandall & Crandall; p.149 right Charles Mann; p.150 Jerry Howard/Positive Images; p.151 Crandall & Crandall; p.152 Design House, Inc.; p.153 top left Crandall & Crandall; p.153 top center Wolmanized® Wood; p.153 top right California Redwood Association; p.153 lower center Kevin Kennefick/Plastival, Inc.; p.154 Storey Communications, Inc.; p.155 top Jerry Howard/Positive Images; p.155 Crandall & Crandall; p.156 Crandall & Crandall; p.157 top ©The Reader's Digest Association, Inc.; p.157 bottom Step2 Company; p.158 Crandall & Crandall; p.159 bottom left Jerry Howard/Positive Images; p.159 top right Sunglo Greenhouse; p.160 Intermediate Malibu; p.161 top center Lambo Products; bottom center silo. Union Tools; p.161 top and bottom right Step2 Company.

ILLUSTRATION

John Hovell Cover art
Elizabeth H. Bartels pages 8,9
Robin Brickman pages 108, 109, 110, 114, 118, 161
Anna Dewdney pages 26, 27, 58, 59, 126, 127, 142, 143
Beverly K. Duncan pages 10, 68, 69, 82, 83, 94, 95
Susan Berry Langsten pages 42, 43
© The Reader's Digest Association, Inc. page 28